# Vincent of Beauvais' 'De Eruditione Filiorum Nobilium':
## The Education of Women

# American University Studies

Series XIV
Education

Vol. 5

PETER LANG
New York · Berne · Frankfurt am Main

Rosemary Barton Tobin

# Vincent of Beauvais' 'De Eruditione Filiorum Nobilium' The Education of Women

PETER LANG
New York · Berne · Frankfurt am Main

Library of Congress Cataloging in Publication Data

**Tobin, Rosemary Barton, 1941–**
  Vincent of Beauvais' «De Eruditione Filiorum
Nobilium».

  (American University Studies. Series XIV,
Education; vol. 5)
  Includes bibliographical references and index.
  1. Women – Education, Medieval.   2. Vincent, of
Beauvais, d. 1264.   De Eruditione Filiorum Nobilium.
3. Education, Medieval – Philosophy – History.
4. Nobility – Education, Medieval.   5. Moral Education –
History.   I. Title.
LC1707.T6   1984      376'.9'02      84-47531
ISBN 0-8204-0105-6
ISSN 0740-4565


CIP-Kurztitelaufnahme der Deutschen Bibliothek

**Tobin, Rosemary Barton:**
Vincent of Beauvais' "De Eruditione Filiorum
Nobilium": The Education of Women / Rosemary
Barton Tobin. – New York; Berne; Frankfurt
am Main: Lang, 1984.
  (American University Studies: Ser. 14,
  Education; Vol. 5)
  ISBN 0-8204-0105-6

NE: American University Studies / 14

© Peter Lang Publishing, Inc., New York 1984

Printed by Lang Druck, Inc., Liebefeld/Berne (Switzerland)

For Jack

namque tu solebas

meas esse aliquid putare nugas

# ACKNOWLEDGEMENTS

    This study of the most important mediaeval treatment of the education of women began some fourteen years ago as a Ph.D. dissertation. My interest in Vincent of Beauvais has continued beyond the appearance of parts of my original statement in JOURNAL OF THE HISTORY OF IDEAS, CLASSICAL FOLIA, HISTORY OF EDUCATION and HISTORY OF EDUCATION BULLETIN, the editors of which I thank for permission to incorporate those parts in the present text. Recent scholarship on Vincent as educator has shown how still vital he is, even if the bolder attempts to find in him the spirit of a proto-humanist are to me ultimately unconvincing. It is my hope that the complete publication of my views will restore the balance in the direction of a much more conservative stance on Vincent's part.

    A number of gifted scholars and teachers have helped me to shape my thoughts. I especially thank Edward J. Power, a wise and patient director; Pierre Lambert, generous advisor; my first Latin teachers, the late Sister Wilfrid du Sacré Coeur Parsons, S.N.D., and Louise Adams Holland; the late Edwin J. Quain S.J. who introduced me to the complexities of mediaeval Latin. I am grateful to Mason Hammond who showed me the glories of classical literature; the late Rolfe Humphries who made clear the poetry of it all; Thomas Corcoran who demonstrated the scholarship needed to preserve the glory; and one very special mentor, Marion Steuerwald.

    My family has been particularly helpful; my mother, Mary M. Barton, has shown me the irreplaceable value of education "in gremio matris", my father, John E. Barton, who with love and support impressed upon me at an early age both the need to work and the central importance of the classical tradition, my lovely daughter, Susannah Barton Tobin, who already has her own views on the education of independent women, and especially, my husband, J.J.M. Tobin, who has offered the best kind of example, has encouraged me at each turn even when he has disagreed with some of my conclusions, and has enriched my every day.

    I wish to thank my students at Emmanuel College for their interest, questions, and desire to know how the story of which they are a later, richer chapter really began. Special tribute goes to Denise Lobb who typed the manuscript with skill and care. Any errors that may exist are, of course, my own responsibility.

Emmanuel College                                    Rosemary Barton Tobin
                                                    Belmont, Massachusetts
                                                    6 May 1984

# TABLE OF CONTENTS

# CHAPTER I

## NATURE OF THE STUDY

This study deals with <u>De Eruditione Filiorum Nobilium</u> of Vincent
of Beauvais, the thirteenth century Dominican encyclopaedist/ed-
ucator, and most specifically with the section of his enchiridion which addresses the education of women. Although studies
of Vincent's general educational philosophy have been made, most
ably by Astrik Gabriel,[1] nevertheless some specific and significant aspects of his thought have received little or no attention. Notable among these neglected subjects is Vincent's attitude toward the education of women. The Dominican devoted the
last ten chapters of his fifty-one chapter didactic work to the
subject of women and their training. The study which follows
offers an analysis and elucidation, with special attention paid
to theme and diction, of Vincent's notions on women's education.
This textual exegesis will be presented within the larger framework of the history of mediaeval attitudes toward the education
of women before the time of and contemporary with him.

The value of this study is two-fold. First, it is the author's hope that this examination will give educational historians some further insight into Vincent's educational thought.
There has been a sad dearth of information about, and elucidation of, this less well-known work of the encyclopaedist. There
are fewer manuscripts of it than of any other work he has written. A great deal of what is known has been based upon imperfect translations rather than upon the original text itself.

For this reason I have made my own translation of the text.
Still less information exists concerning the section of the treatise which deals with women. Even Gabriel's study devotes only
five pages to the question of women. There is much more to be
said. Secondly, it is equally the author's hope that the following chapters will offer a worthy addition to the literature
on the history of women's education. In these days of renewed
interest in women's rights it is important that the scholar ex-
amine carefully the background of the problems and the historical substance both of the movement's concerns and those of all
disinterested scholars.

The book itself contains five chapters which follow this
section devoted to introductory matters. Chapter II will set
the stage by presenting the history of the mediaeval attitudes
toward the education of women with which Vincent would be most
familiar. Chapter III deals with the more formal aspects of the
work: its nature and structure as a kind of literature as well
as its assumptions and presuppositions regarding its audience.
Chapters IV and V contain an analysis of and commentary upon the
content of the section devoted to women. Rather than divide the
analysis of Vincent's views into the three states of womanhood,
maid, wife and widow, I have offered a dichotomous division of
intellectual and moral aspects of those views. The dichotomy
is established by Vincent himself in Chapters 42 and 43, so that
they naturally form a single chapter of discussion. Chapter V
then is devoted to Vincent's Chapters 44-51 which are supportive
and illustrative of the main division treated in Chapter IV.

Chapter VI provides a summary of those discoveries made in the body of the book, in the hope of clarifying the degree to which Vincent does or does not enlarge or transcend the bounds of the conservative structure of mediaeval educational thought.

This author has had the good fortune to have as a Latin text the critical edition made by Arpad Steiner published in 1938 by the Mediaeval Academy of America. This text is based upon three manuscripts, two of which I have examined in Paris at the Bibliothèque Nationale. The third is in the Staatsbibliothek in Munich. Of the two in Paris the B.N. 16390, marked P is the one reproduced in the Steiner edition. It is the oldest of all the manuscripts, (Daunou lists seven manuscripts of De Eruditione in the Histoire Littéraire), composed as it was in the thirteenth century. It is extremely difficult to read, a fact which makes one's debt to Steiner very great indeed. It is much less attractive and legible than the younger and terribly incorrect B.N. 16606. Having stressed primary reliance on the Steiner edition this author must go on to say in all justice that W.E. Craig in his 1949 doctoral dissertation[2] produced several strictures against the total reliability of Steiner. Craig worked from microfilms and did not have the opportunity, as this author has had, to see just how crabbed and well nigh illegible B.N. 16390 truly is. Accordingly he is less appreciative of Steiner's achievement than he might otherwise be. His chief objection is that Steiner has imprecisely placed quotation marks around scriptural citations, yet he is able to say: "Despite its numerous errors, the great bulk of the Steiner text is not apparently in error, and with due caution is available for further educational and historical study."[3] This author concurs, adding only the caveat that the Rev. Mr. Craig's translation of the text, while sober and clear in general, has certain readings which are somewhat misleading, a fact which is surprising given the obvious care with which the work has been done.

Regarding previous studies of Vincent, one full-fledged work is an as yet unpublished doctoral dissertation written at Harvard by John Ellis Bourne in 1960. It deals with Vincent's educational thought, giving very little attention to the education of women. What it does offer in that regard is so strikingly derivative as to undercut any particular significance its relatively recent date might promise. The most thorough-going critical work which uses Steiner as a text is that of Astrik Gabriel originating from the Mediaeval Institute at the University of Notre Dame. His monograph on Vincent's educational theory published in 1956 pays little heed to the education of women. His most singularly provocative paragraph is that: "The last nine chapters of De Eruditione Filiorum Nobilium are devoted to the education of girls. Vincent's educational theory on this subject relies almost entirely upon St. Jerome's Letters to Laeta, Eustochium, and Salvinia, and he quotes at length from St. Cyprian's De Habitu Virginum. He proves himself a worthy forerunner of Christine de Pisan in pleading for the enlargement of women's life."[4] Just what Gabriel means by 'pleading' is moot, but it is the hope of this work that it will demonstrate the truth or falsity of that third sentence, with something to

offer regarding the logic of putting sentences three and two
together.

Joseph M. McCarthy in the most recent full-scale study of
Vincent, <u>Humanistic Emphases in the Educational Thought of Vincent of Beauvais</u>, concludes that Vincent is a classicist and
"proto-humanist". My own disagreement with this view will be
clear to the attentive reader.

Dora Bell in her monograph, <u>L'Idéal Ethique de la Royauté
en France au Moyen Âge</u> has a section on Vincent but hardly mentions the training of princesses. Of the earlier scholars, J.
Bourgeat and Échard made the greatest contributions, but both
are quite out-of-date and neither one spends any time on the
subject of women and their education.

In the area of special topics Pauline Aiken is very in-
trigued by the influence of Vincent upon Chaucer and B. L. Ullman is concerned with Vincent's use of mediaeval <u>florilegia</u>.
There is in addition the use made of Vincent as a structural
principle by Emile Mâle in his celebrated <u>L'Art Religieux de
XIIIe Siècle en France</u>.

In the area of literature dealing specifically with women
in the Middle Ages the Galatea Collection of books on the history of women at the Boston Public Library furnished the otherwise hard to come by Hentsch book on didactic literature addressed to women in the Middle Ages, <u>De la Littérature Didac-
tique du Moyen Âge, S'Adressant Spécialement aux Femmes</u>. My
own appreciation of the variety of critical approaches has been
increased by my use of the valuable work of Carolly Erickson and

Kathleen Casey, "Women in the Middle Ages: A Working Bibliography," _Mediaeval Studies_ 37 (1975), 340-359. No two scholars writing on women in the Middle Ages have been quite so helpful as Eileen Power and Joan Evans especially in their respective works, "The Position of Women" in the _Legacy of the Middle Ages_ and _Life in Medieval France_. In addition there are two other French works of interest, A. Jourdain's _L'Éducation des Femmes au Moyen Âge_ and Rousselot's _Histoire de L'Éducation des Femmes en France_. The author is particularly indebted to F. L. Utley for his book, _The Crooked Rib_, and W. J. Ong's brilliant article, "Latin Language Study as a Renaissance Puberty Rite."

The investigations which follow are designed to determine just how enlightened or unenlightened Vincent's pedagogy truly was. From the very outset it should be borne in mind that the education which is discussed by Vincent is primarily moral, rather than intellectual, and certainly not physical. Further, that moral education is primarily concerned with the problems of concupiscence in maids, wives and in widows, the only acceptable categories for women in the Middle Ages, or those who have responsibility for maids, wives and widows. Regarding the audience of these strictures by Vincent, it should be noted that it is triple in nature: explicitly or implicitly, he has matter for the tutor, the taught, and the royal parents of the taught. It is, moreover, worthwhile to recall that this education is being offered to lay people by a cleric. The thrust of this education towards celibacy is thus understandable from the very beginning, given the vocation of the author.

The most striking aspects to a modern reader of De Eruditione Filiorum Nobilium are the decided moral quality of the education in part and in whole and the remarkably non-academic or
non-institutionalized nature of this instruction.  The former is
understandable given the priestly nature of the author and the
heightened religious sensibility of his immediate audience.  The
latter is equally so once we clarify our own picture of the
structure of mediaeval education.  If we add ethical to the aes-
thetic stress in the following, the nature of training and instruction of the period becomes clearer.

> Rashdall thought that mediaeval university education was
> too dogmatic yet too disputatious, and that if these coup-
> les cancelled each other, imagination (moral as well as
> aesthetic), taste, the sense of beauty were neglected. But
> this is to restrict education to the doings of schools and
> their like.  The Middle Ages did not so restrict it.[5]

Given the moral thrust to the education in general and its
non-institutional setting, we are better prepared to understand
the near total focus on the private, moral instruction of girls
in the concluding chapters of the work.  At the outset, one must
accept the force of the position articulated by Philippe de Novare, a contemporary of Vincent of Beauvais,  in his les
Quatre Tens d'aage d'ome, a vernacular expression of our author's Latin view:

> Women have a great advantage in one thing; they can easily
> preserve their honour, if they wish to be held virtuous,
> by one thing only.  But for a man many are needful, if he
> wish to be esteemed virtuous, for it behooves him to be
> courteous and generous, brave and wise.  And for a woman,
> if she be a worthy woman of her body, all her faults are
> covered and she can go with a high head wheresoever she
> will; and therefore it is no way needful to teach as many
> things to girls as to boys.[6]

The implied inferiority of women and the consequent narrowness of the scope of their education are accepted in large part by Vincent, but the interest we have in the work as a text embodying mediaeval attitudes with barely a hint of enlightenment (with a small 'e') lies precisely in his acceptance only in large part, not in its entirely.

In pursuing these investigations I have kept uppermost in mind the need to focus on both text and context. In terms of the latter, effort has been made to read all the available known studies of Vincent which relate him to the Zeitgeist of which he was so luminous a part. As for the latter, the examination of Vincent's own work in an immediate and particular way has been based on my own original translation of the text. As for other translations, except in those one or two instances where the fame and/or elegance of the version made it an act of supererogation, if not immodesty, to alter them, I have made minor necessary adjustments, chiefly of syntax.

Vincent has a large and a deserved reputation as a scholar and educator. In the past the sheer bulk of his works has been an impediment to close analysis. De Eruditione Filiorum Nobilium unlike the Specula is not three times the length of the Bible; it is a far smaller work, yet there are those who think its importance in educational history belies its relatively modest size. The following chapters attempt to show in just such analysis the nature of that importance.

FOOTNOTES TO CHAPTER I

[1]Astrik L. Gabriel, The Educational Ideas of Vincent of Beauvais (Notre Dame: Mediaeval Institute 1956).

[2]William E. Craig, Vincent of Beauvais, On the Education of Noble Children. Translated from medieval Latin with notes and an historical introduction (Ph.D. dissertation, University of California at Los Angeles, 1949).

[3]Craig, p. 21.

[4]Gabriel, p. 38.

[5]J. W. Adamson, "Education", Legacy of the Middle Ages (Oxford: Clarendon Press, 1969), p. 285.

[6]Eileen Power, "The Position of Women", Legacy of the Middle Ages (Oxford: Clarendon Press, 1969), p. 404.

# CHAPTER II

## ASPECTS OF THE ZEITGEIST RELATIVE
## TO WOMEN AND TO EDUCATION

> Mais qui soulèvera jamais le voile qui cache les origines
> de Vincent de Beauvais?[1]
>
> Vincent de Beauvais est un de ces hommes dont l'histoire,
> malgré leur grande célébrité, a été écrite avec le plus de
> négligence. Les souvenirs que l'on en a conservés sont
> obscurs et incertains pour la plupart. On ignore jusqu'à
> la date de sa naissance et de sa mort, et l'on est dans
> la même ignorance sur son origine et sa véritable patrie.[2]

One wonders when surveying the biographical data on Vincent
of Beauvais why his life is shrouded in such mystery. How is it
that the friend and confidant of Louis IX and the advisor to the
royal family can be virtually lost to us? The Dominican author
of our mediaeval enchiridion, De Eruditione Filiorum Nobilium,
born c. 1190[3] gives himself the appellation Bellovacensis[4] and
is thereby thought to have come from Beauvais. Perhaps it is
with pride in his townspeople that he flourished this epithet,
recalling Julius Caesar's[5] reference to their influence, courage
and great numbers as well as their famous (some would say infamous) surrender to the Romans, that he links himself to his
birthplace. At any rate he is generally known as Vincent of
Beauvais due primarily, if not exclusively, to his own self-
styling.

Vincent became a Dominican sometime before 1220[6] but very
little else is known of his life save what relates to his link
with Louis IX, Saint Louis, and the royal family. The Dominican's magnum opus, Seculum Maius, was dedicated to Louis who

lent both moral and financial encouragement to the endeavor.
The king offered and gave monetary assistance for the copying of
manuscripts, thereby becoming an early example of the patron of
humanistic research.

The king made Vincent a lector[7] at the Royaumont Monastery
which he had founded in 1228 not far from Paris on the Oise.
Our encyclopaedist seems to have been a lecturer on theology for
the monks, a court preacher, and research worker. He was not
himself a teacher but rather what we would call an educational
consultant, a sort of pedagogical expert for the royal family.
So close was he to the family, or so he would have us believe,
that he called himself in that regard domesticus, familiaris.[8]
Or was he simply the family librarian?[9]  In any event Vincent
seems to have been close enough to the king and the family to
have written a consolatio (hackneyed though this custom had become once the consolation was an accepted literary genre) upon
the death of one of the children in 1260.[10]

Whatever his relationship to the royal family it is note-
worthy that he was chosen from all the people who could have
composed a moral enchiridion (handbook or manual), the rationale
of which was to aid in the education of the royal children (Louis, 1244-60 and Isabelle,1242-71).  He wrote De Eruditione Filiorum Nobilium in response to the request of Queen Marguerite
and dedicated the work to her.  That he had not been, as some
have thought, the actual tutor of the royal children,he makes
clear in the preface to the work.  Vincent tells us that he simply transmitted his ideas to the actual tutor, one Simon, a man

otherwise unknown to us. Vincent was, in sum, a theoretical educator rather than a classroom teacher.

Vincent died in his home in Beauvais in 1264[11] if the usual interpretation of an obscure epitaph is correct[12] and if we can trust the statement of Luis of Vallodolid (d. 1436), and an historian familiar with the archives of Saint-Jacques.[13]

> Frater famosus, humilis, plus ac studiosus corpore formosus,
> sapiens ac religiosus.[14]

He is sometimes called Bishop by scholars. This response is probably due to a confusion of him with a Bishop of Tours who died in 1270.

The paucity of facts available to us makes his life but imperfectly known. It is a frustration scarcely to be borne, for here is a man at the eye of the intellectual crosswinds of what has been called the greatest of centuries. Giants of thought in education were his exact and rough contemporaries. In the absence of definite biographical information we are held back from surmise and hope only by the solid and unchanging texts, the great Specula and of course the Enchiridion itself. We must count on these texts for further information about our author.

Vincent's Speculum Maius is a perfect exemplum of the triumph of scholasticism. He is not merely an encyclopaedist who excerpts, but an interpreter as well, giving emphasis to his ideas by a hierarchical positioning of information stressing at all times the relationship of knowledge to the supernatural. The Speculum is a typical product of the scholastic approach but it was not the only one.[15]

Vincent had his predecessors and imitators but part of his importance lies in the accident of his birth. Living as he did at a crucial time, he wrote at the very moment when education was in ferment and when scholastic organization of knowledge became complete. "He forms the watershed between discoverers and organizers on the one hand and popularizers on the other."[16] As we shall see, this view, while correct, is incomplete, for Vincent had aspects of originality not usually associated with either encyclopaedists or popularizers.

The life of Vincent has three foci which often overlapped in his career--the university (Paris), the order (Dominican), and the court (King, later Saint, Louis IX). Born about 1190, Vincent would most likely have gone to the great university at the age of fourteen or fifteen where his studies for the baccalaureate degree would have involved the tried and true trivium of grammar, logic and rhetoric with some elements of the quadrivium, a course later to be outmoded by scientific discovery and research. Paris in 1205-1210 was a university recently granted territorial legitimacy by King Philip Augustus and soon to be awarded Papal approval by the greatest of the thirteenth century popes, Innocent III, who as Lorenzo Conti a decade earlier was a Master of Arts at the very school.[17] The Papal support guaranteed a degree of intellectual freedom in the university far greater than that known in the cathedral schools[18] which were under the supervision and jurisdiction of the local bishop or archbishop. Thus Vincent was a student at Paris after the soon-to-be Pope Innocent and before the golden days of the for-

ties and fifties when Albertus Magnus, Bonaventure, and Aquinas
were teaching (it is a charming irony of history that both Bonaventure and Aquinas proceeded to the Master's degree in 1257).
Vincent narrowly missed the arrival of the mendicant orders in
the university in 1222 and 1223, the Franciscans and his own
Dominicans. Of the celebrated mediaeval scholars who most likely were classmates of the young Vincent, the greatest is Robert
Grosseteste, Franciscan and Oxonian who was at Paris from 1209-
1214. The significance of that chronological parallel is that
Grosseteste lectured on the Ethics of Aristotle--and it is the
presence, however submerged, or absence of those Aristotelian
ethics which greatly interests us in the Enchiridion, especially
those aspects dealing with women.

Whatever it was Vincent learned at Paris, he seems not to
have forgotten his attachment to the mother of all learning, for
if theology was queen of the sciences, the university was regina
sapiens Lutetiae, and here we might duly note the reference to
the university as a woman and a queen. In addition he would
have noted that the days when a teacher could establish by himself the requirements for courses leading to a degree, establish
the manner of presentation and adherence--now there were codi-
fied rubrics as to time, text, examination and degree--a change
which was to become extremely relevant and operative in the life
of Vincent, as we shall see,[19] long after he had left the gown
and the town for the court. What he no doubt took for granted
was the complete absence of women amongst both the faculty and
the student body at the University of Paris.

Sometime after his graduation Vincent entered one of the
two greatest mendicant orders, the order of the Friars Preacher-
in  the folk etymology, the dogs of God, the Dominicans, who
afterwards were to number in their ranks the greatest mediaeval
philosopher and theologian, Thomas Aquinas.  The most significant aspect of Vincent's having entered this particular order is
that the Dominicans' "whole raison d'être was to learn and
preach theology, for which end they were the first to perfect a
system of higher education throughout their order; and from
early days they had a conception of all knowledge as forming a
body of ascertainable truth."[20]  This confidence in the predica-
table and discernible totality of truth led Vincent into the
tradition of the encyclopaedists, whose most famous exemplar
was Isidore of Seville,[21] in a way which allowed him to become
the most universal of universalists, the most encyclopaedist of
encyclopaedists.  Thus Vincent was in keeping with the thrust
of Dominican education, an  education which he had begun in his
pre-ordination days at the University of Paris.  The tensions
between university and order were not to become exacerbated until long after Vincent had met King Louis, at a time when he
had become not only educational advisor to the princes and princess, but spiritual counselor to their parents and a prime religious influence upon the court itself.

The collision between secular masters within the university
and the mendicant orders' scholars was not surprising.  The
attractiveness of the university was directly the result of its
having its own rules and powers free from episcopal control.

When the mendicant orders, both Dominican and Franciscan, entered the university as students and teachers the autonomy of the
university was threatened, for the statutes and by-laws which
had a binding effect upon the secular theologians, masters and
students were ignored or violated by the Franciscans and Dominicans whose ultimate allegiance was to their respective orders.
In the face of the superior discipline, numbers--and some would
say--excellence of the Friars, the secular masters addressed
an open letter to the leaders of Christendom in 1254 against
the mendicant orders in their capacity as university members.
King Louis IX, afterwards canonized as St. Louis, ruled in favor
of the Friars against the seculars.[22]  His judgment was in part
a reflection of the view of his spiritual confessor, a Dominican,
a friar, none other than Vincent of Beauvais.  The Pope, Innocent IV, unlike his predecessor in that name and not an alumnus
of a university, supported the secular masters, but upon his
death in 1254, his successor, Alexander IV, revoked Innocent's
bull which had revoked all privileges hitherto enjoyed by the
mendicants.  In its stead he issued a bull of his own "Quasi
lignum vitae" declaring that the friars were to be admitted to
all rights and privileges enjoyed by other members of the university.  As a result the secular master dissolved the university.  Ultimately the seculars accepted the ruling though they
called the bull "lignum mortis."

It is of high interest that, with the backing of the king,
Vincent should have supported his order against the view of the
then reigning Pope, although what we can make of his judgment,

in terms of the ultimate mediaeval question of the reciprocal
relationship of pope to king remains uncertain. Quite certain,
however, is the fact that Vincent's loyalty to his order forced
upon him conflicts of interest which are reflected in his views
on the role of woman.

At court Vincent found or was picked by--and this is an un-
solved but radically significant issue--a most attractive, warm,
and some would say, soft ruler, who had benefitted from his
mother's administration and his own extreme good fortune. One
senses a reciprocity of view, a mutuality of sensibility between
confessor and monarch. The king was famous for his sense of
justice, and his religious intensity led him to spend and lose
his life on crusade. This sense of justice and religious commitment is manifest in the Enchiridion itself. Whatever the reciprocal relationship of the legendary and historical pairings
of Arthur and Merlin, Charlemagne and Alcuin, Elizabeth and
Ascham, it is clear that Louis and Vincent were an educational
match.

Established as Vincent was with royal support, there are
still several issues of the time which deserve examination.
Prime amongst these is the role of woman in society. Those who
have read Henry Adams' Mont St. Michel and Chartres and Marina
Warner's Alone of All Her Sex know of the cult of the Virgin and
the enhancing fallout from that concept.

Whatever Vincent's response to the "new" Aristotle, basically his Physics and Metaphysics, and the propriety of teaching
the same,[23] from the old Aristotle, the Ethics and Politics, he

would have been exposed--as indeed everyone was in those days

when Aristotle was the Master of those who know--to several as-

pects of a significantly negative view of women.

The first reference in the _Politics_ to women occurs as late

as Chapter 13 of Book I at the conclusion of a discussion of the

household as a segment of the state.  It is in keeping with the

attitude later expressed by Lord Chesterfield in the eighteenth

century that women are but children of a larger growth.

> For these are all matters pertaining to the household and
> every household is part of a state; and the virtue of the
> part ought to be examined in relation to the virtue of the
> whole.  This means that children, and women, too, must be
> educated with an eye to the whole constitution of the state
> --at least if it is true to say that it makes a difference
> to the goodness of a state that its children should be good
> and its women good.  And it must make a difference; for
> women make up half the adult free population and from chil-
> dren come those who will become citizens and participate
> in the political life.[24]

In addition to the pairing of children and women, it is impor-

tant to note the theme of moral goodness being associated with

women.  All too often the flourishing of this theme is thought

to be Biblical, indeed especially Christian; it ought not to be

forgotten that there is this Classical attitude which reinforces

that of Scripture--and doubtless did in the mind of our author,

Vincent of Beauvais.

The last reference to woman reduces her still further from

a level of parity.  In his discussion of the evils of democracy

--and one does well to recall that Vincent was the agent of a

monarchy, equally as predisposed as the Stagirite to disapprove

of the rule of the people--

> Moreover there is something characteristic of democracy in

> all typical features of tyranny--lack of control over
> slaves (which may be expedient up to a point), lack of
> control over women and children, and allowing everyone
> to live as he pleases.  These are the backbone of this
> kind of constitution; most people prefer to live un-
> disciplined lives, they find that more enjoyable than
> obedience to authority.[25]

However, thirteenth century Paris was not quite fourth century

Athens, so that Vincent has no references to slaves and where

one might think him content to compare women with serfs, he does

not.  Far from it, in spite of the pressure of Aristotelian the-

ory, Vincent's own thought and practice independently show a

remarkable similarity as will be seen later.[26]

Between these two references there is one reference to wom-

an which contains a theme present in Vincent's treatment of wom-

an and her roles.  Aristotle is discussing executive officers in

the state upon some of whom devolves the need to "control women".

Although Vincent never uses the word control, he does deal ex-

tensively with the theme of proper authority.  Aristotle wrote:

> Controller of children, controller of women, and officers
> with duties similar to these are aristocratic not democra-
> tic; for who could prevent the women of the lower classes
> from going out when they want to?  It is not oligarchic
> either, for the wives of oligarchic rulers are rich and
> pampered.[27]

The 'controlling' of women with all the pejorative connota-

tions for the female gender in society and indeed, in essence,

was a theme Vincent could easily appreciate.  He could appreci-

ate it not only as a man, not only as a priest, but as a man,

a priest and a Dominican.  It is with his membership in the Or-

der of Preachers that the key to many of Vincent's preconcep-

tions about the essence and role of woman is to be found.

In the course of their preaching--and their preaching reflects their philosophy--the mendicants, both Dominican and
Franciscan, showed a remarkable puritanical streak in regard to
women's dress, cosmetics and vanity in general--all of which
vices were necessarily conducive to eternal perdition and therefore to be condemned by husbands and fathers (and ghostly fathers a fortiori).  Thus the Dominicans "in spite of their greater contact with daily life, showed no advance upon the outlook
of a thousand years of monasticism."[28]  The abbey of Royaumont
was not Mount Athos, but the attitudes concerning mulieribus at
times (and I want to insist upon the modifying force of "at
times") seem identical.

One clear explanation for this excessive stress on female
vanity can be found "in the conventional mediaeval contempt for
women, which regarded them practically as lower order of crea-
tion."[29]  It shall be pointed out below how this view was only
one side of the coin.  Furthermore, it has been correctly, but
not perfectly, stated that "dominated by the celibate clerical
outlook, the Church always possessed a narrow masculine point of
view and far from granting any kind of equality to women, regarded them alternately as objects of scorn and derision or as
so many living temptations always trying to draw men down to
perdition."[30]  Wives could be such vehicles of damnation, and
even for a king.  For the Dominicans, and it is important to
notice their numbers and roles in the circle of Louis IX-- not
only Vincent as court theoretician, but also his confessor and
his tutor, appointed by Blanche, were Dominicans--held a most

rigorous view of connubial love which they passed on to Louis

so that we have such poignant and pathetic scenes as:

> The theologians of the thirteenth century (and the chief
> theologian--indeed the greatest in some sense are Domini-
> cans) were generally opposed to marital relations except
> for the specific purposes of procreation, and sanctity was
> primarily defined as avoiding the urges of the flesh.
> Louis as king had to marry and produce children--he actu-
> ally had a very large family--but that was all, and Marg
> rite suggests that this asceticism was not easy for him.
> The queen later told her confessor that the king, when
> tired with work, often used to come and sit with her and
> the children for a little recreation. Sometimes she no-
> ticed that while he was talking to her, he would not look
> at her, and she was afraid that she might have offended
> him. When she asked him if this was the case, he said no,
> but that a man should not look on that which he could not
> possess.[31]

Vincent of Beauvais need not be credited with having in-

stilled this singular view in Louis, but his own order placed

a particularly high premium on the need to beware of the temp-

tations of the flesh. The general presence of fellow monks

within the abbey and the rather restricted diet of the monks

were helpful factors in limiting both the opportunity and de-

sire for the satisfaction of concupiscence. Further, Dominicans

held that their dress was symbolically significant--and, of

course, none of the Dominicans was more interested in symbolism

than Vincent--as can be seen from the striking significance of

the Specula in the light of Mâle's researches:

> By that wollen inner tunic...which is worn right next to
> the skin without the softness of linen underneath, tem-
> perance is symbolized, the temperance that should be ap-
> plied to the body directly like the inner garment so that
> the concupiscence of the flesh may be restrained.
>
> The same writer found the double cincture, the outer belt
> of leather and the inner band of woven cloth, a token of
> the double chastity of mind and body.[32]

Vincent was not quite so subject to the pressures of com-
munal living and mutual observation both by virtue of his frequent extra-cloisteral visitations to the court and the fact
that as lector at Royaumont he would have had a modicum of pri-
vacy,[33] but there is no reason to assume that he was any the
less careful of the dangers of the flesh than his brethren. Even
when travelling to and from the cloister he would have benefitted from special rules:

> Normally the friars enjoyed the privacy of their cloister.
> But their apostolate obliged them to leave its peace and
> go into the world. There dangers of many kinds beset them,
> especially temptations against chastity. To protect them,
> monastic tradition and Dominican law forbade friars to
> travel alone. The friar must always provide a suitable
> companion. Furthermore, the lawmakers of the Order cau-
> tioned the friars to avoid unnecessary conversation and
> familiarity with women, to shun needless visits to their
> homes, to deal with them only when the ministry demanded.
> Superiors were exhorted to appoint only mature and pru-
> dent friars to hear confessions of women.[34]

Indeed, apart from his important exposure to a special
class of women, which as we shall see did modify his view of the
nature and roles of the gender, Vincent shows no striking facets
of attitude in any way different from other Dominicans. Sad to
say, the adjective most frequently used to modify 'mulier' in
the anti-feminist sermons of the Dominicans is 'fatua', stupid
or foolish, in the sense of not just culpable ignorance but essential weakness. Sadder still is the fact that in the very De
Eruditione the adjective applied all too frequently to woman is
'fatua.'

It is clear that Vincent, whatever he was to learn from
contact with royal women, started with quite negative judgment

concerning women in general simply on the basis of the classical tradition stemming from Aristotle and the sacerdotal celibate tradition particularized and intensified by Saint Dominic. Vincent of Beauvais, priest, student of Artistotle, Dominican lector--and yet a teacher of women. What are we to expect of such a theoretician!

First we should understand that there are three aspects of life which seem quite positive with regard to women and it is to them that we must look to place Vincent firmly in a fair and exact context--for because of the curiously restricted education of Vincent of Beauvais, he later was to offer limited insights into woman's essence and role.

These three areas are politics, theology, and court literature, and in each the domination of women is clear, recognized and accepted.

A most important political fact in Vincent of Beauvais' lifetime was the regency of Blanche of Castille, and the most important figure in the lives of the generation previous to Vincent was that remarkable personage, Eleanor of Aquitaine. The grand-niece was almost as vigorous as the great-aunt, so much so that Joinville (himself the product of an able and domineering mother) was able to state, "King Louis always hid himself when, in his wife's chamber, he heard his mother coming."[35] Blanche was regent twice, first in the minority of Louis (and for the first years of his majority she continued to rule) and later during his first crusade. Against the most varied and dangerous opposition she maintained and solidified the role of the

monarchy in the first half of the thirteenth century. It can
scarely be imagined that Vincent was oblivious to the energy and
accomplishments of Blanche, especially insofar as he was right
in the court with her.

At times both Blanche, and before her, Eleanor, seem to have
the qualities of the termagent or virago, but the truth seems to
be they were no more irascible and dynamic than some kings, indeed "the French woman of the Middle Ages was a masculine character."[36]  Garrou writing in 1899 on the Social State of France
during the Crusades goes further in his analysis of the single-
ness of mores in the Middle Ages:

> A trait peculiar to this epoch is the close resemblance be-
> tween the manners of men and women.  The rule that such and
> such feelings or acts are permitted to one sex and forbidden
> to the other was not fairly settled.  Men had the right to
> dissolve in tears, and women that of talking without prud-
> ery...if we look at their intellectual level, the women ap-
> pear distinctly superior. They are more serious, more subtle.
> With them we do not seem dealing with the rude state of
> civilization that their husbands belong to...As a rule,
> the women seem to have the habit of weighing their acts;
> of not yielding to momentary impressions.  While the
> sense of Christianity is more developed in them than in
> their husbands, on the other hand they show more perfidy
> and art in crime...
>
> One might doubtless prove by a series of examples that the
> maternal influence when it predominated in the education
> of a son gave him a marked superiority over his contem-
> poraries (cf. Freud on that child who is the indisputable
> favorite of his mother is given that sense of confidence
> which itself conduces to success.)  Richard Coeur-de-Lion,
> the crowned poet, artist, the king whose noble manners and
> refined mind in spite of his cruelty exercised so strong
> an impression on his age, was formed by that brilliant
> Eleanor of Guienne who, in her struggle with her husband,
> retained her sons as much as possible within her sphere of
> influence in order to make party chiefs of them.  Our great
> St. Louis, as all know, was brought up exclusively by
> Blanche of Castille; and Joinville, the charming writer so
> worthy of St. Louis' friendship, and apparently so superior
> to his surroundings, was also the pupil of a widow and regent.[37]

Even the friars who complained so bitterly about the near
constitutional immorality of women were careful to cite the un-
failing sanctity which belonged to their own mothers.[38]

Michelet, the greatest of nineteenth century French historians, tried to explain away the success of Blanche on the
grounds that circumstances were perfectly suited to guarantee
the success of the monarchy. He points out that the Church,
particularly the bishops of Sens and Beauvais, and Blanche con-
spired to make the royal widow regent, full in the face of the
argument that no testimony is recorded by Louis VIII or indeed
in terms of logic that he would have appointed a Spaniard ruler
of Frenchmen, never mind a woman to boot. Yet he provides the
very liabilities--woman, widow and foreigner, liabilities which
Blanche overcame. And even Michelet is forced by historical
fact to cite the instances of maternal regency: Blanche, of
course, but also Marie, Countess of Champagne, Jane, Countess
of Flanders and Isabella of Marche. He adds in a footnote that
in 1250 there was a female sultan, _mirabile_ _dictu_.

Although obviously disapproving of such a monstrous regi-
ment of women, of such female hegemony, Michelet, as Garreau
and Henry Adams after him, had to in all integrity describe what
had indeed happened. If Michelet and the others at such a distance recognized the pervasive rule of women, how much the more
so must have Vincent who lived in the very midst of it all.
Further, he must have noticed that these female regents were
all widows--a fact which led him to accept the more readily St.
Jerome's[39] tripartite division of the life of a woman: maid,

wife, widow, when he came to write De Eruditione.

If politics told Vincent the force and equality of women, theology only stressed the woman's superiority, or at least one woman's superiority as maid, mother, and widow. The thirteenth century is the high water mark of the religious phenomenon, 'maryolatry'--and the great art form of the Middle Ages, the Gothic cathedral (to which Vincent contributed so much on the theoretical level in his Speculum Maius) was built for her.

Perhaps politics and theology are related, for we all tend to explain the unknown in terms of the known. Mary, like Blanche was an all powerful queen (and it is most fitting that the great rose window at Chartres was donated by Blanche), simply raised to an infinite degree. As Adams put it so well in terms of the effect of this maryolatry on the world: "How passionately they worshipped Mary, the Cathedral at Chartres shows; and how this worship elevated the whole sex, all the literature and history of the time proclaim."[40]

The parallel of an all powerful intercessor-like woman with a young or weakened son is common to both the Blessed Virgin Mary and Blanche of Castille, and perhaps Michaelangelo's Pietà, but represents the relative vigor of mother and son. It is also true that when Blanche died, and certainly by 1270 when Louis himself passed on, the zenith of maryolatry had passed, but it did so after the death of Vincent in 1264 so that our author knows only the dominance of the Virgin in the theological and architectual world and that of the regent mother in the socio-political realm. Whatever his study of Aristotle and his life

as a Dominican had told him about the capacities of women, the
larger experience of life told him quite the opposite. A striking piece of evidence of Vincent of Beauvais' awareness of this
maryolatry is found in the following:

> More popular ideas of the Virgin Mary's power over her Son
> are exemplified by Caesarius' story of the simple-minded
> Cistercian lay-brother who was heard to pray, 'In truth,
> Lord, if Thou free me not from this temptation, I will com-
> plain of Thee to Thy Mother.' The comment was much edified
> by the lay-brother's simplicity, and by our Lord's humility
> in condescending to grant a prayer couched in such terms.
> We have here only the grosser side of the rapidly-growing
> materialism: the great encyclopaedist, Vincent of Beauvais,
> who compiled his work with the help of St. Louis' library,
> writes of a Pope as saying that 'Mary, the Mother of Jesus,
> ..is the only hope of reconciliation for (sinful) man, the
> main cause of eternal salvation.'[41]

One other sphere of culture was dominated by women, and
that an area oddly pedagogical. Because it more than balances
the negative picture of women presented in the literature of the
fabliaux, something should be said of the secular religion of
courtly love and its perverted but feminine exalting of religion.

The fabliaux are humorous and scurrilous tales centering
on bawdy anecdotes, represented in England by Chaucer's "Mil-
ler's" or "Reeve's Tale." In all these efforts women's promis-
cuity and cunning are displayed at every opportunity. Even
though the weaknesses of priests are the object of ridicule almost as much as the foibles of women, it is not likely that Vincent was particularly familiar with the fabiaux,[42] for the genre
itself is bourgeois and middle-class, and Vincent was nobly de-
scended. Far more likely he was familiar with the traditions of
courtly love. The greatest poet of the tradition was Chrétien
de Troyes and the spiritual ruler of it was Marie de Champagne

(both Troyes and Champagne are close to Beauvais) and the celebrity of Provençal song was all that was left of southern culture after the devastating crusade against the Albigensian heresy in 1209.

Going back to the days of Eleanor of Aquitaine and Marie of Champagne, just as Vincent was born, there was that great opportunity of female dominance as a result of their husbands' absence by death or continous military maneuvers. The most favorable interpretation of the resulting code of love was that, however ennobling in its by-products, it was essentially an adulterous system. Henry Adams finds a parallelism, odd to say, existing between maryolatry and courtly love:

> While the Virgin was miraculously using the power of spiritual love to elevate and purify the people, Eleanor and her daughters were using the power of earthly love to discipline and refine the courts. Side by side with the crude realities about them, they insisted on teaching and enforcing an ideal that contradicted the realities...Eleanor... Marie...and...Blanche...used every terror they could invent as well as every tenderness they could invoke, to tame the beasts around them. Their charge was of manners, and, to teach manners, they made a school, to which they gave the name of 'courteous love.'[43]

This is not simply a matter of literature, but of life--and Blanche was viewed as a heroine of romance, with her Isolde being answered by the Tristan of Thibault of Champagne. Vincent could scarcely approve of a cult of secular love, and he did not live long enough to see Dante fuse aspects of the Blessed Virgin Mary and the rarified lady in the Divine Comedy; nevertheless he noticed that courtly love offered women as teachers, men as the taught and used a textbook (the De Arte Honeste Amandi of Andreas Capellanus). In examining Vincent's De Eruditione, it is im-

portant to notice these questions of teacher, taught, and text
in terms of gender.

In review, Vincent inherited both negative and positive attitudes toward women, their nature and roles. The negative he
inherited from his studies of classical writers like Aristotle,
the older mediaeval culture, and most particularly from the attitude of the Dominican order. The positive he acquired from
the political, theological and then current cultural achieve-
ments of women.

It may now be asked were there already existing specific
statements regarding the instruction of women. "Already" is the
key word. Of course there were the letters of St. Jerome, but
the two best known treatises specifically devoted to the education of women in the Middle Ages were written slightly later
than the lifetime of Vincent. They are the _Livre du Chevalier
de la Tour Landry_ (1371-72) and the _Menagier de Paris_ (1393).
The former was directed towards the author's own noble (although
not royal) daughters, yet suffers as a possible analogue to _De
Eruditione_ by reason of its quite lax morality, which, though
it makes as much of the use of examples as Vincent, borders often on the risqué. The latter, for all its charm with its vi-
gnettes of domestic singing and dancing, is so bourgeois and so
limited to a young wife's instruction, that it can hardly serve
as a later parallel to _De Eruditione_.

More helpful are those scattered hints and examples which
are found before and during the lifetime of Vincent: such factors as those recorded by Powicke and Emden in their revision of

Rashdall:

> Early in the thirteenth century Florence provided many of
> the dictatores or stylists of Bologna, and a hundred years
> later its arithmetical schools through their textbooks in-
> fluenced teaching north of the Alps. Lay teachers are
> found from 1275 and included a married woman, Clementia,
> doctrix puerorum (1304) who could teach the rudiments of
> Latin.[44]

Some of the significance of this fact, a significance which is
not restricted simply to the bolstering the maternal-offspring/
teaching-learning relationship, will be noticed later.[45]

Even before the Florentine lady Latinist, there were women
at Paris trying to enter the medical faculty. Rashdall himself
points out:

> It is curious to see the 'medical woman' questions fought
> out in a prosecution directed by the medical faculty at
> Paris against a woman who had cured the royal chancellor
> and many others for whom the physicians could do nothing.
> She alleges inter alia that 'mulier antea permitteret se
> mori quam secreta infirmitatis sue homini revelare.'[46]

Rashdall, of course, fell into the notorious gaffe about
the mythical women doctors of Salerno, led by Dame Trot, but he
does point out two interesting Spanish contributions to women's
education which though after Vincent, perhaps accurately reflect
the Spanish contribution of previous days--and one does not forget that Blanche, the Queen of France, was first and foremost,
Blanche of Castille. First he quotes Graux: "The privileges of
a Spanish university--those of Lerida in 1300--are almost the
only ones with which I am acquainted, which expressly contem-
plate married undergraduates."[47] And Rashdall himself is rather
surprised when he is led to the following conclusion of a later
time.

> Salamanca is not precisely the place where one would look
> for early precedents for the higher education of women.
> Yet it was from Salamanca that Isabella the Catholic is
> said to have summoned Dona Beatrice Galíndo to teach her
> Latin long before the Protestant Elizabeth put herself
> to school under Ascham. The Renaissance man, indeed, he
> considered to have begun in Spain long before it began
> in England.[48]

Now Vincent is not the Renaissance, nor frankly, the start

of an incipient Renaissance, but there was increasing interest

in the education of women in the Middle Ages, an interest which

can best be summarized despite the dearth of complete and numer-

ous texts as being more expansive than restrictive. The best

evidence of fresh influence comes from an unexpected source, a

most exceptional Dominican, Humbert, the fifth general of the

order, and one who had, it appears, a profound influence on Vin-

cent not simply in urging him to finish his work on royal gov-

ernment (left unfinished still at his death). Humbert had a

strong appreciation of all learning to the point where he was

able to relate knowledge and wisdom to the theme of _nosce te_

_ipsum_: "For whosoever knows most, the better in consequence he

will know himself, which is of greatest usefulness to man."[49]

Humbert's interest in the education of girls is quite startling,

given St. Dominic and his successors' aversion and hostility to

women. Humbert's views are clearly stated in materials for the

sermon titled _For Girls or Maidens Who Are in the World_:

> Just as it is praiseworthy in Christ to preach to boys
> (a notion charmingly taken up by Colet and Erasmus in his
> sermon, _On the Child Jesus_), so it is also an act of cha-
> rity to instruct girls in the faith when the opportunity
> occurs, either in their schools or at their homes or wher-
> ever else they be. Note that these girls, especially if
> they be the daughters of the rich, ought especially to
> devote themselves to study, for to this purpose their par-

> ents have intended them.  Hence they ought to know the
> Psalter or Hours of Our Lady or the Office of the Dead
> or other prayers to God, and so be more fitted for reli-
> gious life should they wish to join it later, or more
> fitted for the study of Sacred Scripture, like Paula and
> Eustochia and others who remained unwedded, and who be-
> cause of their devotion to books became deeply versed in
> sacred letters.  Of this knowledge you have an example in
> Blessed Agnes who went to school , in Blessed Cecelia,
> Catharine, Lucy, Agatha, who were all learned as their
> legends bear witness.  Let them, therefore, not be solic-
> itous about their clothes ...let them beware of levity in
> dance or song or game...let them fear men.  Let them take
> some good spiritual man to be their father whose counsel
> and teaching shall rule them...let them be at home with
> their parents and grandparents, not wander astray from
> their homes.[50]

Having praised Humbert for his interest in the education of
women, we should now say that while he thinks education is a
desideratum for girls, the goals and curriculum of that education are remarkably narrow.  Yet with the shortage of positive
texts we must be grateful for even Humbert.  A better indication, from the point of view of the scope of women's education,
comes not from an influence on Vincent of Beauvais, but from one
whom he is said to have influenced through his work De Eruditione.
Indeed, this discussion of the tradition of feminine education
in the Middle Ages can be concluded best with a citation from
Christine de Pisan in rebuttal to Thomas Aquinas (naturally e-
nough a Dominican and an Aristotelian) who had said that only in
generation was woman a helpmate to man:

> I reflected why men are so unanimous in attributing wick-
> edness to women.  I examined my own life and those of other
> women to learn why we should be worse than men, since we
> also were created by God.  I was sitting ashamed with bow-
> ed head and eyes blinded with tears, resting my chin on my
> hands in my elbow-chair, when a dazzling beam of light
> flashed before me which came not from the sun, for it was
> late in the evening.  I glanced up and saw standing before
> me three female figures, wearing crowns of gold and with

radiant countenances. I crossed myself. Whereupon one of
the three addressed me: 'Fear not, dear daughter, for we
will counsel and help thee. The aphorisms of philosophers
are not articles of faith but simply the mists of error
and self-deception.'[51]

FOOTNOTES TO CHAPTER II


[1]Marie Dominique Chapotin, Histoire des Dominicains de la
Province de France (Rouen: Imprimerie Cagniard, 1895), p. 356.
"But who will ever lift the veil which hides the origins of
Vincent of Beauvais?"


[2]J.J. Bourgeat, Études Sur Vincent de Beauvais (Paris:
Auguste Durnat Libraire, 1856), p. 18. "Vincent of Beauvais
is one of those men whose biography has been treated with
negligence in spite of great fame. The information which has
been preserved is obscure and uncertain for the most part. We
are ignorant as to the date of his birth and of his death and
there is the same ignorance concerning his origin and his true
home."


[3]Ibid., p. 17.


[4]Ibid.


[5]J. Caesar, Gallic War, II, 4. "Plurimum inter eos Bello-
vacos et virtute et auctoritate et hominum numero valere."


[6]Bourgeat, p. 17.


[7]Bourgeat, p. 18.


[8]P. Feret, La Faculté de Théologie de Paris et Ses Docteurs
Les Plus Célèbres (Paris: Picard et Fils, 1895), p. 405.


[9]Feret, p. 405.


[10]The Epistola consolaria was sixteen chapters in length,
elaborating upon the futility of worldly interests and stressing
the joy of the dead who had found heaven. See Epistola consola-
toria in Opuscula ed. cit. Basel, 1481.


[11]Bourgeat, p. 21.

[12] B.L. Ullman, "A Project for a New Edition of Vincent of Beauvais," Speculum, 8 (1933), p. 312.

[13] However, Tholomaeus de Luca, Vincent's younger contemporary (d. 1321), believed him to be alive during the pontificate of Gregory X (1271-76). We do know that he was alive in 1260 when he wrote the Tractatus Consolatorius upon the death of Louis, the heir, but I agree with most scholars who place his death in 1264.

[14] Histoire Littéraire de la France, 18 (1895), p. 458. "A celebrated brother and a humble one, devout and assiduous, wise, and pious."

[15] More well known representatives of this approach are Abelard's Sic et Non and the Sentences of Peter the Lombard.

[16] R.R. Bolgar, The Classical Heritage and its Beneficiaries (New York: Harper & Row, 1954), p. 235.

[17] One avoids here any discussion of the profound impact of anti-feminism in Innocent's De Contemptu Mundi.

[18] A greater degree of stability too was evidenced in the university than that which we observe when first one cathedral school and then another comes into prominence, depending upon the reputation and personality of its head.

[19] See below, pp.

[20] David Knowles, The Evolution of Medieval Thought (New York: Vintage Books, 1964), p. 256.

[21] Isidore of Seville (c. 570 - 636) wrote an encyclopaedia, Etymologiae or Origines which treated everything he considered worth knowing from the standpoint of etymology.

[22] Knowles, pp. 232 - 33.

[23]In 1231 at Paris a committee was established to purge the books of Aristotle but in 1255 the faculty of arts prescribed the forbidden books.

[24]T.A. Sinclair, trans., _Aristotle's Politics_ (Baltimore: Penquin Books, 1962), pp. 53-4.

[25]Ibid., p. 185.

[26]See below Chapter IV and V.

[27]Sinclair, p. 244.

[28]R.F. Bennett, _The Early Dominicans_ (Cambridge: University Press, 1937), p. 121.

[29]Ibid.

[30]Ibid.

[31]Margaret Wade Labarge, _Saint Louis_ (Boston: Little Brown & Co.,), 1968, p. 211.

[32]William Hinnebusch, _The History of the Dominican Order_ (New York: Alba House, 1966), p. 134.

[33]G.R. Galbraith, _The Constitution of the Dominican Order_ (Manchester: University Press, 1925), p. 184. (See the constitutional stipulation: "The friars were all to sleep together. Only the master-general could, if the accommodations of the house allowed it, have a room for himself. A 'lector' might have a separate room if the prior thought it would help his work.")

[34]Hinnebusch, p. 137.

[35]Henry Adams, _Mont-Saint-Michel and Chartres_ (New York: Mentor, 1961), p. 195.

[36]Adams, p. 192.

[37]Ibid.

[38]Joan Evans, Life in Medieval France (New York: Phaidon, 1957), p. 29.

[39]Implicit in letters to Laeta and Eustochium.

[40]Adams, p. 246.

[41]C.G. Coulton, From St. Francis to Dante (New York: Russell and Russell, 1907, reprint 1968), p. 119, cites Vincent's Speculum Historiale VII. 95.

[42]See Margaret Schlauch, English Medieval Literature and Its Social Foundations (Warsaw: Panstwowe Wydawnictwo Naukowe, 1956), especially Chapter 12, pp. 270 ff.

[43]Adams, p. 206.

[44]Hastings Rashdall, The Universities of Europe in the Middle Ages (a new edition by Powicke and Emden, Oxford: University Press, 1936), vol. II, p. 47.

[45]See also the intriguing qualifications this has with regard to W.J. Ong, S.J.'s celebrated essay, "Latin Language Study as a Renaissance Puberty Rite," Studies in Philology, LVI (L959), pp. 57-75.

[46]Powicke and Emden, vol. I, p. 424.

[47]Ibid.

[48]Ibid.

[49]Bede Jarrett, O.P., *Social* *Theories* *of* *the* *Middle* *Ages*
(New York: Frederick Ungar, 1966), p. 31. It should be pointed
out also that the friars' condemnation of frivolity never refers
to learning as frivolous, although this is most likely a function
of the class of the friars' audience and its considerable lack
of literacy.

[50]Ibid., p. 87. There were indeed schools for girls, but
in Paris in 1272 there were a dozen schools for children, eleven
of which were for boys and only one for girls. These schools
offered tuition quite modest and often free to the children of
the city or the town. The curriculum consisted primarily of the
first levels of religious instruction, although sometimes the
rudiments of Latin and even Greek were taught. In the twelfth
century it was, however, chiefly in the monasteries (sic) that
the girls of the middle and upper classes received their education. Most of these female students were taught the three R's,
plus music. Some few of them learned enough Latin to understand
the canon of the mass, to read the Bible, the Fathers of the
Church and those poets and historians deemed to be morally edifying. St. Louis, cognizant of the tragic effect his Crusades
had on those family members left behind by husbands and fathers,
inquired of the widows of those who fell in the Crusades whether
or not their daughters knew their 'letters'--and made arrange-
ments that these girls and also those who were completely orphaned receive an education at the abbey of Pontoise, or elsewhere. Although at least one writer has, on the basis of the
success of the Dominican study plan with the twin readers, bibi-
licus and sententiarius, called St. Dominic 'the first minister
of public instruction in Europe', it is to the realm of private
instruction that Vincent belongs. Beginning in the thirteenth
century many noble and upper middle class parents decided against
sending their daughters to monastery schools in favor of private
tuition at home. This instruction was given either by female
teachers or 'Latiners,' clergymen who also assisted the family
chaplain (and here we see that Vincent's position was too lofty
for him to consider the actual tuition of royal children--he
remained properly, by social standards, the overall theoretician
of their education). Their curriculum included religious lessons,
basic Latin--and significantly for the future, French, music,
literature and surprisingly, some rudiments of medicine. It
might be pointed out that many of the male royal members dictated
their ideas to clerks who put them into Latin, but the female
members did their own writing--and that it was basically in
French. This opening of the Pandora's box of the vernacular will
be discussed in a later chapter, especially as Marguerite, mother
of Vincent's charges, had a role in the movement. Many of these
girls, shut out from the universities, gained whatever higher
education they were to receive as members of a convent. It has
been argued that the number of learned abbesses was equal to the

number of abbots of intellectual distinction. Vincent of Beauvais had particular reason to admire these ladies for they not
only were distinquished copyists of manuscripts but "les cou-
vents abritaient aussi des poetes, des historiennes, des ency-
clopedistes, des moralistes, des epistolieres, des savantes."
Anyone who has tried to make a true precis or proper abridgement
will understand the intelligence required for such activity.  To
conclude this explanation, there was serious if minority education for girls in the twelfth and thirteenth century France,
both public and private, and it is to the latter that Vincent
primarily belongs.

Concerning the copyists mentioned above, a radically important factor is that of the oral tradition within which they
worked.  We make the mistake of thinking that the scribe copied
as we today--in the absence of a handy Xerox machine--might
easily reproduce with little effort of eye and hand a short
text.  "This was certainly not the case, for the reason that we
gain the majority of our information and ideas from printed matter, whereas the mediaeval obtained them orally.  He was con-
fronted not by the beautiful productions of a university press,
but by a manuscript often crabbed in script and full of contrac-
tions, and his instinctive question when deciphering a text was
not whether he had seen, but whether he had heard this or that
word before; he brought not a visual but an auditory memory to
his task.  Such as the result of his up-bringing; he had learnt
to rely on the memory of spoken sounds, not upon the interpretation of written signs.  And when he had deciphered a word, he
pronounced it audibly."  Chaytor (From Script to Print, p. 14)
then illustrates the truth of this judgment in a fascinating
footnote: "The process is thus described by a copyist of the
eighth century on concluding his work: qui scribere nescit multum putat esse laborem.  Tres digiti scribunt, duo oculi vident.
Una lingua loguitur, totum corpus laborat, et omnis labor finem
habet, et praemium eius non habet finem' . . . Three fingers
hold the pen, the eyes see the words, the tongue pronounces them
as they are written and the body is cramped with leaning over
the desk.  The scribe is obviously unable to avoid the necessity
of pronouncing each word as he deciphers it."

[51]Ibid., pp. 84-85.  It is not so much my purpose to conclude with an obvious example of women's rights as it is to illustrate something of the tradition within which Vincent worked
and to which he added.  I would like to point out that Christine's dates are 1364-1430, that is, she was born a century after Vincent.  This fact should underscore the paucity of documents relating to mediaeval educational theory and still further,
given a gap in time, how much less likely it was that Christine
would have been influenced directly by the writing of Vincent
to any appreciable degree.

# CHAPTER III

## THE STRUCTURE AND EXPECTATIONS
## OF DE ERUDITIONE

In this chapter investigating the formal aspects of De Eruditione, as well as the presuppositions which Vincent has made regarding both the text and those to be taught, the following
chain of argument appears:  first, Vincent uses Latin rather
than French and he expects his students to do the same; second,
the Latin texts to be read are classical as well as scriptural;
third, classical texts are derived from compendia, often compendia with glosses such as Vincent himself used; fourth, exempla drawn from both classical and scriptural texts imply a
measure of ignorance on the part of either Vincent, his audience, or both; fifth, both classical and scriptural  texts are to
be read allegorically, and sixth, these exempla, with their
arguments and authorities, make up the three-pronged weapon of
Dominican preaching.  De Eruditione is fully as much a sermon as
it is a treatise.

At the same time that Vincent was expressing in Latin his
views on the essence of women's education, Philippe de Novare
was in his les Quatre Tens d'Aage d'ome, arguing in the vernacular rather much the same position.  In part this stated, "Women
have a great advantage in one thing; they can easily preserve
their honour, if they wish to be held virtuous by one thing only."[1]  Yet by his very language Vincent with his Latin seemed to
have been demanding more of the royal female students. Philippe,

on the other hand, wrote in French. During the Middle Ages, according to Ong:

> vernacular literature tended to be regarded as literature
> for women, who were mostly denied formal schooling, that
> is, denied the Latin which would have opened the philosophy
> and science books to them. Hence, the importance in ver-
> nacular history of romances and devotional books and ser-
> mons for mixed audiences.[2]

Vincent was writing for a mixed audience. The examples he uses suggest that the children as well as the tutor were to read or hear the treatise, and he was particularly interested in de-votional material and sermons. Yet if the boys were to have the Latin to read the works of science and philosophy, indeed to read his own encyclopaedic works, so were the girls. It is a matter of considerable importance that Vincent should have used Latin and avoided the French.

Within the treatise permission is given to some students to read Latin texts, and these Latin texts are both classical and scriptural. In so doing Vincent is not unique. With this use of the classical writers by Vincent it is important for us to understand that whatever distinctive quality there is belonging to our author, he was working within that mediaeval, encyclo-paedist tradition begun by Isidore of Seville. It was Isidore who established a Christian theory of literature by using an interesting systematic schemata of chronology. Isidore held that the poetic genres of antiquity stemmed from Israel, so that ipso facto they were legitimized from the Christian viewpoint. Sacred and secular books could thus be set side by side without the necessity of making value judgments. In his presentation

of a doctrine of the primacy and prerogative of Israel in philosophy, science and poetry, Isidore's "poetics" integrates the
doctrine of pagan antiquity into the systematized didascalium
of the Western Church.  His writing thereby acquired an importance which can hardly be overestimated--especially insofar as
it led to the viewpoint of the last and greatest of the encylo-
paedists, Vincent of Beauvais.  Easy as it is to see this con-
tinuation of the tradtion by Vincent, more difficult to appreciate are other equally vital aspects.

There are several difficulties in determining precisely
Vincent's personal position on particular matters of education.
These stem from his adoption of the widespread use of florilegia,
glossae and patchwork quotation.  This last is especially relevant to his use of Jerome, himself a practitioner of quotation
by a cut-and-paste method which also features unacknowledged or
misleading borrowing.  The result of this practice is a palimp-
sest of ideas, the responsibility for each layer of which is
not always easy to determine.  Nevertheless the selection and
use of these layers are original to Vincent of Beauvais and are
his responsibility.  The order and arrangement of the ideas are
totally his and so to a lesser degree are the modifications he
inserts.  Whatever Vincent's accomplishments as an original
thinker, it is clear that Steiner is most certainly incorrect,
as we shall show below, in his judgment  that, "over one sixth
of all citations are drawn from Jerome, on whose ideas the education of girls is entirely based."[3]

Florilegia, about which all too little is known at present,

are further obstacle to a clear determination of the viewpoint
of the writer making use of them.  Further, they cast strong
doubts about the writers's direct knowledge of classical texts.
The alleged classicism and sometimes consequent humanism of certain mediaeval writers turns out to be a mistaken reflection of
such secondary sources.  It is known that Vincent made use of a
twelfth century work called the _Florilegium Gallicum_ from which
he drew many more prose than poetry quotations (as did John of
Salisbury from his Carolingian _florilegium_).[4]  Vincent quotes
St. Jerome so often we forget that sometimes he quotes him directly and sometimes from a _florilegium_!  The chief result of
derivative citation is that half-truths are produced whose effect would be to vitiate the argument they illustrate, were the
other half but known.  Below we shall consider three examples
of Vincent's mistaken use of florilegial figures which show that
either Vincent was ignorant or that he was counting on the ignorance of his audience.  It will be recalled that his audience
was a threefold one:  the tutor, the royal pupils, and the royal
parents.

     As for _glossae_, they allow for still further distancing of
the writer from the ideas he is presenting.  They may be his i-
deas but they are so by acceptation rather than by creativity.
These glosses were a necessary function of the manuscript econ-
omy of the Middle Ages.  With few texts of the Church Fathers
and later commentators available, such texts as did exist were
copied onto the Bible (Vulgate, of course) either interlineally
or more frequently marginally.  Thus by a kind of incremental

repetition the ideas, historical and theological, as well as linguistic, of Jerome, Augustine, Ambrose et al. were preserved in a conceptual _florilegium_ such as the most famous of these collections, the ninth century _Glossae Marginales_ of Walifridus Strabus who added also the comments of Isidore, Bede, Alcuin and himself. It should be patent from the foregoing that the line separating tradition from the original contribution of Vincent is not always discernible. This is a problem exacerbated by Vincent's casually ambiguous mode of quotation and his encyclopaedic instinct to include as much previous material on any topic as possible.

Vincent's reliance on such secondary sources produces some oddities of illustration in the course of his argument. That he would use _exempla_ to make his views clear is natural enough, the time immemorial practice by good teachers of making the abstract concrete, but it was particularly incumbent upon him as a Dominican and a preacher to be as illustrative as possible. His advisor and superior, Humbert of Romans, had urged their use and so famous did these _exempla_ become that in the fourteenth century in a secular manner the child wife of the Menagier de Paris was instructed by them. At that later date they involved eccentric stories drawn from unnatural natural history and speculation about demonic meetings with the faithful, but in the beginning of their widespread use by the Dominicans there were literal instances of Biblical and historical morality. Jerome and Gregory the Great used them and the latter especially urges their use in "sunt nonnulli, quos ad amorem patriae caelestis plus exempla, quam praedicamenta succendunt."[5]

Humbert of Romans was most specific as to the kind of teaching exempla which should be used. Although these rubrics are found in a treatise on preaching, it will be allowed that Vincent's work in De Eruditione Filiorum Nobilium is a form of education preaching with a power beside that of the pulpit. Humbert asserts that the exempla must be "of competent authority lest they be held of no account; they must also possess some likelihood so that they may be believed, and they should be edifying lest they be recited to no purpose."[6] These exempla could be drawn from pagan classics as well as from the Bible, the grounds established by St. Augustine or the authority of the Apostle Paul: "Nam quid aliud fecerunt multi boni fideles nostri? Nonne aspicimus quanto auro et argento et veste suffarcinatus exierit de Aegypto Cyprianus et doctor suavissimus et martyr beatissimus? Quanto Lactantius? Quanto Victorinus Optstua, Hilarius, ut de vivis taceam? Quanto innumerabiles Graeci? Quod prior ipse fidelissimus dei famulus Moyses fecerat, de quo scriptum est, quod eruditus fuerit omni sapientia Aegyptiorum."[7]

It is within the framework of these Egyptian spoils that Vincent's pedagogical thrust seems to have exceeded his grasp, without doubt as a result of his too confidently or too carelessly trusting in his secondary sources and the ignorance of his audience. The first of these tactical errors occurs in Chapter 43; after quoting Jerome to the effect that man as well as woman should work for the health of his soul he then says:

Sed et Suetonius etiam in libro II de XII Caesaribus dicit

quod et Augustus Caesar 'filiam et nepotes ita instituit,
ut etiam lanificio assuefaceret ac loqui vel agere quicquam
nisi palam et quod in diuturnos vel diurnos referretur
commentarios vetaret.'[8]

Of the three criteria urged by Humbert, Vincent easily sat-
isfies the first two: 'the competent authority' is Suetonius,
and if Vincent's historical acceptance of this sensationalist
historian is uncritical, it is true that Suetonius was one of
the auctores accepted as a quarry from which to mine exempla;
second, "some likelihood that they be believed" is satisfied by
the unusual, but by no means incredible, picture of an emperor
turned domestic tutor. However, it is on the third and most important desideratum that Vincent fails: "they should be edifying
lest they be recited to no purpose." It is incomprehensible to
the knowledgeable reader of today that Vincent could have been
so eccentric in his choice of exemplum here. The infamy of the
two Julias, the daughter and granddaughter of Augustus, is well
known. Suetonius spells it out in Book II, Chapter 65, the very
next chapter, where a scant dozen lines after this homey tableau
come: "Julias, filiam et nepotem, omnibus probris contaminatas
relegavit."[9] Then adding a wayward grandson to the bad examples
of daughter and granddaughter, after quoting Homer to the effect
that he wished he had remained unwed and childless, Augustus,
according to Suetonius "nec aliter eos appellare quam tris vomi-
cas ac tria carcinomata sua."[10]

What are we to make of this startling choice by Vincent of
Beauvais? Was the teacher ignorant? Possibly, but John of
Salisbury knew Suetonius at first hand and he seems, after

Sallust, to have been the most influential of Roman historians upon mediaeval historiographers.[11] Did the teacher count on the ignorance of the student? Possibly, but what would guarantee the preservation of that blissful ignorance? Controlled reading is the answer or, not to put too fine a point on it, censorship. Florilegia themselves are a form of censorship--and they are a part of the tradition of Christian education that goes back to Augustine whose theories made viable the parallel judgments of Jerome. It was Augustine who saw the advantages of the principle of selection and the use of the compendium. Compendia were Augustine's way of adhering to the principle set down by Juvenal "maxima debetur puero reverenter." Vincent it seems followed this restrictive, linguistically destructive but morally helpful technique. It may well be that Vincent's knowledge of Suetonius was limited to some such compendium or florilegium, but it is likely that he expected the knowledge of his students to be even more limited.

It is a fact, true and sad, that the paucity of manuscripts, indeed the total absence of manuscripts of certain authors, prevented writers like Vincent from achieving their desired ends more smoothly. If there had been a Tacitus for Vincent of Beauvais instead of a Suetonius, how much more effective and more apposite would Vincent's exempla have been:

> Every citizen's son, the child of a chaste mother, was from
> the beginning reared, not in the chamber of a purchased
> nurse, but in that mother's bosom and embrace, and it was
> her special glory to study her home and devote herself to
> her chilren. It was usual to select an elderly kinswoman
> of approved and esteemed character to have the entire
> charge of all children of the household. In her presence

> it was the last offense to utter an unseemly word or to do
> a disgraceful act. With scrupulous piety and modesty she
> regulated not only the boy's studies and occupations, but
> even his recreations and games. Thus it was, as tradition
> says, that the mothers of the Gracchi, of Caesar, of Augustus,
> Cornelia, Aurelia, Atia, directed their children's education
> and reared the greatest of sons.[12]

This is quite perfect for Vincent had Vincent but known it:
Tacitus was an _auctor_ among the Romans fully equal to Thucydides
among the Greeks, but alas, "mediaeval historians could not read
Thucydides and they did not read Tacitus. . ."[13] According to
Bolgar:

> Many classical books, however, were available only in large
> libraries or in jealously guarded private collections, while
> such authors as Catullus, Lucretius, and Tacitus whose sur-
> vival through the middle ages had depended on rare isolated
> manuscripts still remained, as might be expected, hidden
> from view.[14]

The second instance of peculiar example, the true nature of
which, if but known, would vitiate the argument it hopes to illuminate occurs in Chapter 47 "On Giving a Girl in Marriage",
"unde refert Valerius Maximus libro VII, quod, 'quidam unice
filie pater Themistoclem consulit, utrum eam pauperi sed ornato,'
sc. moribus 'aut locupleti parum probato collocaret. Cui ille,
'malo,' inquit, 'virum pecunia quam pecuniam viro indigentem.'"[15]

Here the lesson is sufficiently edifying, the instance ac-
ceptably probable, but the authority in the immediate text is
suspect. Valerius Maximus is the source and the multiplicity
of _exempla_ in his work, _Factorum et Dictorum Memorabilia_ made
him an especially attractive source for our author, However,
Themistocles, apart from the fame or infamy of his having taken
refuge at the hearth of his enemies was a singularly odd choice

for moral judgments with regard to young ladies and marriage.
Plutarch wrote: "In the first essays of his youth he was not
regular nor happily balanced; he allowed himself to follow mere
natural character, which, without the control of reason and instruction, is apt to hurry upon either side, into sudden and vi-
olent courses. . ."[16] And regarding his maturity, Themistocles,
again according to Plutarch, seems to have condoned domestic
connections bordering on the Egyptian. "He had many daughters,
of whom Mnesiptolema, whom he had by a second marriage, was wife
to Archeptolis, her brother by another mother; Italia was married to Panthoides, of the island of Chios; Sybaris to Nicomedes
the Athenian. After the death of Themistocles, his nephew,
Phrasicles, went to Magnesia, and married, with her brother's
consent, another daughter, Nicomache, and took charge of her
sister, Asia, the youngest of the children."[17] Of course Vincent does not use Plutarch, who seems almost unknown in the Middle Ages, and therefore missed seeing the other works which
might have helped him in the education of women "Coniugalia
Praecepta" and "Consolatio Ad Uxorem." Here at least we may
say that Vincent's ignorance matched that of his audience, so
that censorship does not have to be implicitly involved.

The last example is scriptural rather than classical: twice
Vincent invokes the example of Judith, the brave widow who slew
Holofernes, though it is not her widowhood which, surprisingly,
is the aspect of focus. Rather Chapter 48 "On The Instruction
Young Girls Should Receive Concerning Married Life" has an un-
impeachable example of Judith from Book X of the work named for

her in which she exemplifies the proper kind of adornment, that
which is an external manifestation of her inward virtues.  Earlier she had appeared in the chapter on the need to avoid excessive ornamentation (Chapter ILIV).  In the midst of a dis-
quisition on the harlot-like wiles of female clothes, eyes, and
posture, Vincent, drawing from the same tenth book says:

> In Hanc bos vel asinus cadit, cum quilibet iustus vel iniustus
> sive sapiens vel stultus eius specie capitur, sicut Holofernes
> statim captus est in oculis Iudith, ut legitur in Iudith X.[18]

Given the largely negative context, there is the possibility of
confusion to the mind of the non-Bible reading audience.  In the
midst of these examples to be avoided there is one which seems
to be encouraged.  Vincent of Beauvais' use of this reference to
Judith suggests strongly that his audience was so well instructed in the Bible, including the Old Testament, that there would
be no difficulty in anyone's mind in determining who was evil,
who was good, and who was so singular in the eyes of God.  It is
a shame that Vincent of Beauvais given his positive attitudes
towards the training of girls should not have included from
Judith XI, 18, 19:  "Placuerunt autem omnia verba haec coram
Holoferne et coram pueris eius; et mirabantur sapientiam eius,
et dicebant alter ad alteram: non est talis mulier super terram
in aspectu, in pulchritudine, et in sensu verborum."[19]  Here the
intelligence of Judith is given equal force with her beauty.

   We know that Vincent is not only a very great transmitter
but a great practitioner of _exempla_, (for unnatural natural history _exempla_ compare the veil and the bear of Chapter XLVIII and
the basilisk of Chapter XLV) but in this work his examples are

drawn ultimately, with the exception of the two oddities cited
in the parentheses, from the Bible and Classics.  There is nothing among his exempla in De Eruditione so outlandish as the figure  of the ursine-bodies, ass-headed Pope Benedict IX of the
Speculum Historiale.  In general, we say that in keeping his
exempla probable and clear, Vincent relied on his audience's
knowledge of the Bible and ignorance of the Classics.  In at
least one case he appears himself somewhat ignorant.  Nonetheless his practice of selective quotation suggests both the need
for present and future censorship in regard to the reading of
the royal children.  The sad truth that all description is necessarily selective (cf. choosing Judith X, but not Judith XI)
implies great responsibility of choice.  The modern reader of
educational history is pleased to see the openness and interest
Vincent has in female education, but he is equally aware that
the opening is far from total.  Nothing shows this limitation
quite so well as Vincent's use of exempla.

Important as are issues raised by the censorship resulting
from qualified selection of exempla, still more important is the
use of allegorical interpretation, interpretation we usually
think of as belonging to the world of poetry and, in the mediaeval world, especially to the works of Dante.  And Dante was born
just as Vincent died.  Both wrote in a tradition which moralized
both Ovid and the Bible.  Augustine it was who so clearly put
into words his solution to the problem "quidquid in sermone divino neque ad morum honestatem neque ad fidei veritatem proprie
referri potest figuratum esse cognoscas" (whatsoever in holy

writ cannot be properly said to be concerned either with morality or with the faith must be recognized as allergorical.)[20]
Thus we may presume that if Vincent had intended girls to read
Sacred Scripture in general and the Song of Songs in particular,
he most assuredly would have had the young ladies see the words
through the spectacles of the allergorical tradition.

As for allowing them to read pagan writers, and most especially his own favorite, Ovid, the same principle would have
been evoked. Unlike Virgil whose fourth eclogue, the messianic,
readily endeared him to Christian thinkers well before Dante
made him his guide through the Inferno, Ovid had a well earned
reputation of being the author of some of the most exceedingly
provocative poems, even handbooks on the art of love, with a
small 'l'. Yet the beauty of her verse and the theme of Meta-
morphoses so endeared him to readers of Christian times that the
same tactics of interpretation which had been applied to Scripture (as indeed it had long before by the Stoics been applied
to Homer) were utilized with him. The best description of the
attitude toward Ovid and the need to clean him up a bit (to the
point of inventing Ovid's conversion by St. John the Apostle)
is the following:

> a mediaeval Latin scholar looked upon the Roman writers and
> especially upon the authors of school texts, the auctores,
> as teachers from whom he could acquire a standard of writing,
> who presented him with the rules of literary technique and
> awoke his creative imagination. But they were also close to
> his heart, and he lived with them as friends. The separa-
> tion caused by the centuries that had passed was forgotten,
> and the barrier between the Christian and the pagan became
> negligible. Such an attitude was accentuated by the idea
> that there had been pagan prophets and by the invention of
> pure fables.

> As late as the 16th century Erasmus, moved by the virtue of
> classical pagans, could say 'Sancte Socrates, ora pro nobis.'
> Already in the 11th century the Christianization of Ovid was
> begun: Manegold of Lauterback maintained that the learned
> poet had outwardly professed faith in the heathen gods be-
> cause he feared the emperors, but that in reality he had
> hidden Christian truth in his works. The melior natura
> in Metamorphoses I, 21 is explained as voluntas dei or even
> filius dei.[21]

When Vincent urges the study of 'ancient letters' as a means of
occupying the time and energy of girls the better to preserve
their chastity, it is important to realize that Vincent was opening a Pandora's box, the lids to which he could easily put back.
As Steiner has properly said,[22] Vincent has many statements concerning the need to read only the most pious of writers, yet in
his own practice he cites fully as many pagan writers as patristic. What was a Dominican pedagogue doing by inviting these
waxen souls to come to the fire? Even the Jesuits[23] at a later
date forbade boys (never mind girls) to read Aeneid IV for its
supposed combustible properties--and one should recall too, that
Virgil is tame stuff compared to Ovid, and Vincent himself
quotes Ovid thirty times more frequently than he does Virgil.
And even if 'ancient letters' means Holy Scriptures rather than
the classics--as is possible, but hardly probable--what was Vincent doing by allowing a girl to read the Song of Songs? The
answer, of course, the lids of this Pandora's box, is allegory.

Whenever texts have proved refractory to accepted morality,
the force of piety has broken the text into levels of meaning.
From the early Hellenistic thinkers well into modern times the
most serious and holy of interpreters have allegorized when
necessary and somtimes when not. We all recall that Dante in

his letter to Can Grande said that the _Divine_ _Comedy_ should be
read on four levels:

> Ad evidentiam itaque dicendorum sciendum est quod istius
> operis non est simplex sensus, potest polisemos, hoc est
> plurimum sensuum; nam primus sensus est qui habetur per
> litteram. Et primus dicitur litteralis, secundus vero
> allegorisus sive moralis sive anagogicus. Qui modus
> tractandi, ut melius pateat, potest considerari in his
> versibus: 'In exitu Israel de Egypto, domus Jacob ex
> populo barbaro, facta est Judea sanctificatio eius, Israel
> potestas eius.' Nam si ad litteram solam inspiciamus,
> significatur nobis exitus filiorum Israel de Egypto tempore
> Moysis, si ad allegoriam, nobis significatur nostra redemp-
> tio facta per Christum; si ad moralem sensum significatur
> nobis conversio anime de luctu et miseria peccati ad statum
> gratie: si ad anagogicum, significatur exitus anime sancte
> ab huius corruptionis servituti ad eterne glorie libertatem.
> Et quamquam isti sensus mistici variis appellentur nominibus,
> generaliter omnes dici possunt allegorici, cum sint a lit-
> terali sive historiali diversi. Nam allegoria dicitur ab
> 'alleon' grece, quod in latinum dicitur 'alienum,' sive
> 'diversum.'[24]

Now Dante had put Statius in Purgatory and wonderfully enough
had put Trajan in Paradise, but one likes best the idea  that
Ovid was not simply a Christian, but a saint. Vincent's girls
were reading the work of a splendidly skilled dirty old man as
if it had been written by Origen.

All of his interpretation was based on attitudes of the
reader rather than the writer--and Vincent sought to control the
expectations of his female readers in order that they would, in
an a priori fashion, find what they wanted to find, rather than
to seek out what the author most likely must have intended.

> The book is independent of its author, as Abelard knew,[25]
> and may quite properly have meanings, under God, which the
> author never intended. Thus one very common way of begin-
> ning an interpretation is 'Istam fabulam intellego'--'I
> understand.' The resulting interpretation is based not so
> much on an empirical analysis of the book itself, even though
> a certain kind of outlining analysis is important, as it is
> upon a priori assumptions about the nature and final cause

of verbal meaning. I can understand Ovid, or Solomon, or
Moses in a certain way because this is the way books are
supposed to be understood.[26]

Of all the works quoted by Vincent regarding allegorical
interpretation, no Biblical text demanded so great a care in
heightening as did the Song of Songs/Song of Solomon/Canticle of
Canticles. From the very beginning of scriptural exegesis the
literal translation/interpretation has been found either contra-
dictory or wanting. From the earliest Hebrew scholars one finds
an interpretation that is far more morally heightening than a
simple literal appreciation. The ancient Talmudic scholars
viewed it as an analogue of Yahweh and Israel.[27] Origen thought
that the groom was Christ and the bride the Church. Bernard of
Clairvaux tended to think of the bride as the Blessed Virgin
Mary. "To the scholastic of the Middle Ages the book was full
of mystic meaning."[28] Even the earliest of the interpreters
tried to have their cake and eat it too. Thus even Origen
thought that "the song might be an epithalamium on the marriage
of Solomon with the Pharaoh's daughter."

In later times Luther was to say that the bride was the
state and thus Solomon was being grateful to his loyal people.
Only in more recent times has the text been treated as literal
and erotic. The only member of the early Church to view it in
a non-allegorical light seems to have been Theodore of Mopsues-
tia: "For this the Church later anathematized him."[30] One
question surfaces in the midst of all this symbolic interpretation: if it is not symbolic "how (did) it ever get into the canon, if it is merely a collection of secular love songs..."[31]

Regarding Vincent of Beauvais, it is important to realize that he, as well as Humbert of Romans, constantly invokes the Song of Songs--and that they are following in the tradition of St. Bernard of Clairvaux, the Cistercian who had written so many works on the Canticle of Canticles. It is important to remember that Vincent, a Dominican, was made lector in a Cistercian monastery: "Meanwhile in 1228 Louis had begun to build the Cistercian monastery of Royaumont, near one of the royal estates. Hearing from the abbot about Vincent's large volume of excerpts, he paid to have a copy transcribed for his own use. Presumably as a result of his approval of this work, Louis appointed Vincent a lector in the new monastery. In this capacity according to Vincent himself, he lectured and preached to the royal family and was asked to write special treatises, of which De Eruditione was one."[32] The issue of the proper interpretation of the Song of Songs is a vexed one, yet in terms of logical consistency one must bear in mind the position of the true believer. The position may be expressed thus: you begin with presupposition; therefore you conclude the words must mean something other than they say. As St. Augustine puts it: "Quidquid in sermone divino neque ad morum honestatem neque ad fidei veritatem proprie referri potest figuratum esse cognosces."[33] So deeply imbued with this readiness to find figurative meaning was Vincent that he is able to count on his audience as having the same response as does he himself. How else to explain the casual confidence he displays in his quotations. Admittedly they are even more outlandish than Humbert of Romans, "Et ideo dicitur Cant. 4: Sicut vitta coccinea labia tua. Quod exponit <u>Glossa</u> de praedicatoribus, qui sunt labia Ecclesiae. Sicut igitur vitta restringit superfluitatem capillorum ita et labia ista cavere debent a superflua prolixitate verborum."[34] Thus in the 45th chapter he quotes Bernard himself on the allegory of humility inherent in the <u>Song of Songs</u>:

> unde in cantico canticorum II dicitur in persona, ipsius, sicut exponit beatus Bernardus: 'cum esset,' inquit, 'rex in accubitu suo, nardus mea dedit odorem suum. Nardus siquidem herba humilis est et pectus purgat. unde manifeste humilitatem designat cuius odor et decor invenit graciam apud deum?'[35]

This is a relatively innocuous text, but the violation of what was to be Occam's razor which is so much a part of the extravagant interpretation is patent in the references to the text which recur throughout <u>De Eruditione</u>.

Finally in this consideration of form and presupposition in <u>De Eruditione</u> the link between the treatise and sermon and Vincent and Humbert should be made stronger.

In viewing Vincent of Beauvais as an educator one must remember that the educational goal of the Middle Ages was <u>salvation</u> of souls, something at times forgotten in our desire to find Renaissance features in early texts. It is helpful to recall that Vincent was a Dominican and that the chief vehicle in the quest for salvation of the souls of others for the Dominican order was in preaching. The form which that preaching takes is the sermon. It is this writer's judgment that <u>De Eruditione Filiorum Nobilium</u> derives its form not simply from the <u>collectanea</u> of one sort or another so characteristic of the

times, but is in fact a sermon.  Besides, one may go further
and suggest that Vincent was a kind of Dominican Isocrates who,
if he for reasons of modesty or weakness did not read his works,
had others vocalize words he wrote.

Consider the role of Vincent within his own order: encyclopaedist yes, link with court, yes, but in terms of specific title he was lector.  The description of the duties of that office
in De Vita Regulari of Humbert of Romans, fifth master of the
Dominicans and thus ultimately Vincent's superior, tells us a
good deal of how Vincent went about his educational task within
the order, a manner we may assume he continued a fortiori without.
Humbert begins:

> officium boni lectoris est conformare se capacitati auditorum,
> et utilia, expendentia eis faciliter et intelligibiliter legere,
> opiniones novas refugere, et antiquas, et securiores tenere;
> ea quae non bene intelligit numquam dicere; a fastidiosa pro-
> lixitate, quae accidere solet ex nimia repetitione eiusdem,
> aut ex involutione verborum, vel ex aliis causis, cavere
> semper.[36]

This concern for both the reader and the audience with the great
stress on humble obedience to the accepted interpretation, and
obedience doubtless congenial to Vincent in his other role as
encyclopaedist gatherer rather than inventor of materials, continues:

> Porro monitiones emanantes a capitulis circa lectores debet
> diligenter retinere in memoria, et servare; licentius vero
> generalibus de loquendo, vel remanendo a choro, et similibus
> non debet uti propria auctoritate, et ad libitum suum: sed
> prout priori visum fuerit et causa rationalibus requisiverit.[37]

This restriction on the lector was designed to preserve his humility and his audience's confidence in certitude of the Faith.
Both elements profited thus within the walls of the convent.

Outside, the sermon had requirements equal to those of the read-

ing. Humbert as the chief preacher of the Order of Preachers

spelled it out in the following ways in his Liber De Eruditione

Praedicatorum:

> Praeterea, homo secundum philosophos est dignissima
> creaturarum: de duabus vero eius naturis, scilicet corpore
> et anima, dignior est anima. Cum vero circa animam multa
> requirantur, quorum quaedam parum aut nihil faciunt ad
> salutem, ut scientia: illa quae pertinent ad salutem
> digniora. Porro praedicatio versatur circa hominem;
> unde Matth. ult, dicitur Apostolis: Praedicate Evangelium
> omni creaturae, id est homini, secundum Gregorium. Non
> autem circa corpus, sed circa animam.[38]

In this definition of the focus of the preacher we find also the

reason for the absence of references in Vincent of Beauvais to

any aspect of physical or bodily education. Mind and soul are

the objects of Vincent's training for 13th century royal/relig-

ous France was no gymnastic Sparta or Juvenalian Rome. It is

a shame that Humbert does not specify that the audience to which

Christ addressed the works interpreted as a description of the

Bible, the support of Preaching, was a woman even if of Samaria:

> A fine, quia aliae scientiae sunt vel ad regimen temporalium,
> ut scientiae iuris; vel ad utilitatem corporum; ut scientiae
> medicinae; vel ad informationem animorum secundum aliquam
> imperfectionem ignorantiae, ut speculativae: haec autem est
> ad vitam aeternam habendam. Joann. 4: Qui biberit ex aqua
> quam ego dabo ei, fiet in eo fons aquae salientis in vitam
> aeternam.[39]

However, Humbert of Romans does provide two early references

to women, the first of which is further material for the need to

understand correctly the mediaeval view of the Song of Songs:

> Iste autem cantus est adeo coram Deo acceptus, sicut etiam
> in curiis magnates solent in cantibus joculatorum cantus
> sponsus dicit Ecclesiae, Cant. 2: Sonet vox tua in auribus
> meis: vox enim tua dulcis. Glossa: Praedicationem volo,
> quia talis vox dulcis.[40]

The second of these is one which for its combination of eccle-
siastical and politcal references must have pleased the heart
of Vincent of Beauvais, Sap. II:

> Domine qui amas animas. Quasi super omnia vero encaenia
> mittuntur ei per praedicationem. Quis ergo posset dicere
> quam accepta sit talis oblatio et cum gaudio recipiat eam?
> Ideo dicitur in Ps. 59: Adducentur per opportunam prae-
> dicationem, afferuntur per importunam. Et sequitur: Af-
> ferentur in laetitia et exultatione: quia cum magno gaudio
> recipietur talis oblatio.[41]

Not only would Vincent have been heartened by the feminine analogies of Humbert of Romans, but he would have been pleased by
the support given, as I say, not only to his audience, but to
his manner, thus:

> Sunt alii qui ad persuadendum quod dicunt, utuntur quandoque
> solis exemplis, quandoque solis auctoritatibus: sed melius
> est uti quolibet istorum ad aliquid presuadendum, ut quem
> non movet unum, moveat aliud, quia multi sunt qui plus
> moventur uno quam alio. Et cum ista tria concurrunt circa
> idem, fit funiculus triplex, ligatus cum hamo praedicationis,
> qui difficile rumpitur a pisce quocumque.[42]

It is the practice of Vincent of Beauvais to follow exactly in
De Eruditione Filiorum Nobilium the triple-functional approach
of example, argument and authority.

To reinforce how influential Humbert of Romans is in terms
of Vincent of Beauvais' practice, consider the judgment of Humbert and the practice of Vincent in the following:

> Unde Augustinus de Doct. Christ. lib. 4: Si regina Ester pro
> suae gentis temporali salute locutura apud regem oravit, ut
> in os eius sermonem congruum Dominus daret: quanto magis
> orare debet ut tale munus accipiat qui pro aeterna hominum
> salute in verbo et doctrina laborat?[43]

Vincent used Esther as an exemplum in Chap. XLVII

> Legitur eciam in Hester, quod ipsa cubile regium introducenda
> muliebre cultum non quaesivit, sed que volint, ab egeo ad
> ornatum accepit. Erat enim formosa valde et incredibili

> <u>pulchritudine</u> omnium oculis graciosa et amabilis videbatur
> . . . et . . . ut legitur in <u>Hester</u> XLII: Tu scis, domine,
> necessitatem meam quod abhominer signum superbie et glorie
> mee quod est super caput meum in diebus ostentacionis nee
> et detester illud quasi panuum menstruate et non portem
> in diebus silencii mei?[44]

Although one hesitates to rely upon the argument <u>ex silen-</u>
<u>tio</u>, it is nevertheless a point well worth considering in terms
of <u>De Eruditione</u> as a sermon and the idea of Vincent as a Dominican Isocrates when we read:

> Item sonoritatem in voce.  Multum enim perit de fructu ser-
> monis, cum praedicator propter vocis debilitatem non potest
> clare audiri.  Ido frequenter in Scriptura sacra vox prae-
> dicatoris, voci tubae comparatur, quia potenter debet resonare,
> et clare ad modum tubae.  Os. 8: In gutture tuo sit tuba; quod
> dicitur praedicatori.[45]

However relatively weak or strong voiced Vincent may have
been, he does follow the practice of the mediaeval preacher by
beginning with a text: in this case <u>Ecclesiasticus</u> 7: "Filii
tibi sunt?  erudi illos et curua illos a puericia eorum.  Filie
tibi sunt?  serva corpus earum et non ostendas hylarem faciem
tuam ad illas" and repeating it at the beginning of Chapter 42.
He then proceeds to flourish these themes by means of examples
drawn from the Classics and the Scriptures, argument strict and
metaphorical, and authority from Themistocles to Christ, pro-
viding subsidiary and supportive themes until the conclusion or
peroration which involves application in a closing formula.
The expansions and dilations of the themes could belong to either treatise or sermon, but the conclusion seems fitting only
to the latter.  There with a delicate touch of withdrawal behind auctorial quotation, yet not wholly extinquishing his in-
dividualism, Vincent cites Cyprian on the need to persevere to

the end of life in moral chastity just as the text itself comes
to an end, without summary or recapitulation but with an appeal:
"O, inquit, sacre virgines, hortamentis vos mutuis excitate,
emulis de virtute documentis ad gloriam provocate durate fortiter, pergite spiritualiter, pervenite feliciter, <u>tantum</u> mementote
<u>nostri</u>, cum in vobis insipiet virginitas honorari."[46]

Moving as this conclusion is, one can see on the basis of
the analysis of this chapter how both the expectations and the
limitations of Vincent's form and manner will qualify the content of <u>De Eruditione</u>.

FOOTNOTES TO CHAPTER III

[1] Eileen Power, "The Position of Women" in The Legacy of the Middle Ages ed. by Crum and Jacob (Oxford: Clarendon Press, 1926), p. 404.

[2] Walter J. Ong, S.J., Ramus: Method, and the Decay of Dialogue (Cambridge: Harvard Press, 1958), p. 11.

[3] Arpad Steiner, De Eruditione Filiorum Nobilium of Vincent of Beauvais (Cambridge: Mediaeval Academy of America, 1939), p. xxiii.

[4] R. W. Hunt, "The Deposit of Latin Classics in the Twelfth-Century Renaissance," in Classical Influences on European Culture A.D. 500-1500 ed. by R. R. Bolgar (Cambridge: Univeristy Press, 1971), pp. 54-55.

[5] "there are some whom exempla inflame more to love of the heavenly land than qualities do." (my translation). Judson Allen, The Friar As Critic (Nashville: Vanderbilt University Press, 1971), p. 45.

[6] Allen, p. 46.

[7] "For what else did our many good faithful ones do? Didn't we see Cyprian and the most delightful doctor and the most blessed martyr leave Egypt laden with so much gold and silver and clothing? And with so much Lactantius and with so much Victorinus, Optstua, Hilarius to be silent about the living? And with so much the innumerable Greeks? First the most faithful servant of the lord, Moses himself, did this, concerning whom it is written, that he was learned with all the wisdom of the Egyptians." De Doctrina Christiana, II, 60-61.

[8] "But, and Suetonius even in Book II of his Lives of the Twelve Caesars says that Augustus Caesar 'taught his daughter and his granddaughter wool making and forbade them say or do anything unless they did it openly and unless it could be recorded in the daily commentary of the house.'"

[9] "He banished the two Julias, his daughter and granddaughter whom he had found tainted with every crime."

[10] "Nor did he refer to them in any way except as his three boils and three ulcers."

[11] Bolgar, _Classical Influences on European Culture, A.D. 500-1500_, p. 165.

[12] _Dialogus De Oratoribus_, 28.

[13] Bolgar, _Classical Influences on European Culture, A.D. 500-1500_, p. 172.

[14] Bolgar, _The Classical Heritage and its Beneficiaries_, p. 262.

[15] "Hence Valerius Maximus in Book VII, The father consulted Themistocles concerning his only daughter as to whether to marry her to a poor man with morals or a rich, unacceptable one. He said, 'I prefer a man lacking in money to money lacking in manliness.'"

[16] Plutarch _The Lives of the Noble Grecians and Romans_, John Dryden, trans. (New York: The Modern Library), p. 134.

[17] Ibid. p. 154.

[18] "Into this pit an ox or an ass falls whenever anyone whether he be just or unjust, wise or foolish, is taken by appearance, just as Holofernes was immediately captured by Judith as one reads in Book X."

[19] "And all these words were pleasing to Holofernes and his servants, and they marvelled at her _wisdom_ and said one to the other: there is not such a woman on the earth in appearance, in beauty, and in the sense of her words."

[20] Basil Willey, _The Seventeenth Century Background_ (New York: Doubleday, 1953), p. 81.

[21]Bolgar, Classical Influences on European Culture, A.D. 500-1500, p. 84.

[22]Steiner, p. xv.

[23]Bolgar, The Classical Heritage and its Beneficiaries, p. 358.

[24]Charles S. Singleton, Comedia, Elements of Structure (Cambridge: Harvard Press, 1965), p. 86.  Mr. Singleton's translation of the above is: "To elucidate, then, what we have to say, be it known that the sense of this work is not simple, but on the contrary it may be called polysemous, that is to say, "of more senses than one"; for it is one sense that we get through the letter, and another which we get through the thing the letter signifies; and the first is called literal, but the second allegorical or mystic.  And this mode of treatment, for its better manifestation, may be considered in this verse: "When Israel came out of Egypt, and the house of Jacob from a people of strange speech, Judea became his sanctification, Israel his power."  For if we inspect the letter alone, the departure of the children of Israel from Egypt in the time of Moses is presented to us; if the allegory, our redemption wrought by Christ; if the moral sense, the conversion of the soul from the grief and misery of sin to the state of grace is presented to us; if the anagogical, the departure of the holy soul from the slavery of this corruption to the liberty of eternal glory is presented to us.  And although these mystic senses have each their special demoninations, they may all in general be called allegorical, since they differ from the literal  and historical.  Now allegory is so called from "alleon" in Greek, which means in Latin "alieum" or "diversum."

[25]Si quis autem me quasi importunum ac violentum expositorem causetur, eo quod minus propria expositione ad fidem nostram verba philosophorum detorqueam, et hoc eis imponam quod nequaquam ipsi senserunt, attendat illam Caiphae prophetiam, quam Spiritus sanctus per eum portulit, longe ad alium sensum eam accomodans quam prolator ipse senserit.  Nam et sancti prophetae cum aliqua Spiritus sanctus per eos loquatur, non omnes sententias ad quas se habent verba sua intelligunt, sed saepe unam tantum in eis habent, cum spiritus ipse, qui per eos loquitur, multas ibi provideat, quatenus postmodum alias aliis expositionibus, et alias aliis inspirat.  (Introductio ad Theologiam I.)

[26]Judson Boyce Allen, The Friar As Critic   (Nashville: Vanderbilt University Press, 1971), p. 61.

[27]The Interpreter's Bible   (New York: Cokesbury Press, 1951-1957), p. 92.

[28]Ibid.

[29]Ibid.

[30]Ibid., p. 94.

[31]Ibid.

[32]William E. Craig, Vincent of Beauvais, On the Education of Noble Children.  Translated from medieval Latin with notes and an historical introduction  (Ph.D. dissertation, University of California at Los Angeles, 1949), p. 3.

[33]"Whatever in a holy sermon cannot be concerned with either morality or the truth of the faith you can recognize to be allegorized."

[34]"And likewise Cant. 4 says: your lips are like red fillets. The gloss of the preachers explains this to be the lips of the Church.  Therefore just as fillets restrain flowing hair, so the lips ought to beware of too lengthy speeches."

[35]"Hence in Song of Songs II it is written, while the king is sitting down, the nard offers its odor.  Indeed, the nard is a lowly herb and cleanses the heart.  For its odor clearly indicates humility and its appearance finds grace with God."

[36]"It is the duty of a good lector to adjust to the level of his audience; to read useful and expedient things easily and intelligibly; to avoid new opinion and to retain older and more secure ones; it is his duty never to say things he doesn't understand well: to always avoid hateful wordiness which comes from too much repetition of the same things and to avoid involuted language and other things."

[37]"Further he ought to have the readers memorize and guard
the warnings which flow from the titles of the chapters; but
with regard to speaking more freely, staying away from the dance
and the like, he should not use his own authority and whim: but
to the extent that it was seen before he ought to seek good
reasons."

[38]"Besides, according to the philosophers, man is the high-
est of creatures, composed of body and soul, of which the soul
is the more worthy and all which concerns its safety must be
given more attention than that which is of little importance to
man.  The preacher concerns himself with the rational man for:
preach the gospel to all men i.e. to man which means the soul
not the body."

[39]"In the end, other sciences are only concerned with the
rule of worldly things, as the science of law is; or the care
of the body, as the science of medicine is; or the instruction
of the spirit according to some imperfection of ignorance, as
the speculative sciences; eternal life ought to be gained from
this; Who drinks of the water which I give him, but there will
grow in him a fountain of water to life eternal."

[40]"And this singing is pleasing to God just as princes are
accustomed to delight in the songs of entertainers, and the
spouse of the Church says: let your voice resound in my ears:
for your voice is sweet.  The gloss says: I want you to be
preaching because such is a sweet voice."

[41]"The Lord loves souls above all.  These above all things
are sent Him by the preacher.  Who therefore can say how and
with what joy such an offering is received?  Likewise it says
in Psalms: these will be brought to you by the preacher in season and out of season.  And they will be brought in joy and
exultation because with great joy such an offering will be received."

[42]"There are others who to be persuasive use only examples
or argument or authority: but it is better to use all three so
that when one is not successful, another may be.  And when the
three are used there is a threefold cord with a fishhook which
is not easily broken by the fish."

[43]"When one reads in Esther that being brought to the king's

bed she did not seek feminine adornment but wished only what
Hegei gave her.  For she, extremely attractive and of incredible
beauty, seemed lovable in everyone's eyes . . . and as we read
in Esther, "you know, Lord, that his is necessary and I loathe
all signs of pride and glory which is on my head in days when
I am displayed, and I hate it as a menstrual rag, and that I do
not use it in private."

[45]"A resounding voice--when a preacher cannot be heard because of the weakness of his voice he will lose much of the
fruit of his speeches.  Likewise frequently in scripture the
sacred voice of a preacher is compared to the sound of trumpets,
because it ought to resound powerfully and in the manner of a
clear trumpet.  May there be a trumpet in your throat.  This is
said to a preacher."

[46]"He said, o holy virgins, stir one another up with encouragement, call to glory with examples of virtue in rivalry,
persevere bravely, go on spiritually, achieve with good fortune,
remember us when your virginity is honored."

# CHAPTER IV

## CHAPTERS 42 AND 43:

## THE BASIC DICHOTOMY OF THE EDUCATION OF WOMEN

Vincent's educational ideas regarding girls are expressed in
Chapters XLII through LI of De Eruditione Filiorum Nobilium. He
begins by citing again Ecclesiasticus, 7.26, the opening Biblical quote of Chapter I, "Filii tibi sunt/ erudi illos et cura
illos a puericia eorum. Filii tibi sunt? serva corpus earum et
non ostendas hyllarem faciem tuam ad illas."[1] Such an opening
quotation with its sources is fittingly traditional and thematically most significant. The tradition lies in the fact that
Ecclesiasticus, the book itself was used in the Roman Catholic
Church from the very earliest days as a text "for the instruction of catechumens and neophytes."[2] At their age the young
princes and princess are at least neophytes, soon to be catechumens in matters of religious education.

Thematically the significance is profound: the boys are to
be instructed and their excessive pride contained; the girls are
to have their vanity controlled and their bodies guarded. Here
we have the key aspect of the education of girls. It is neither
physical nor intellectual but primarily moral. And morality is
circumscribed by a narrow definition which refers primarily to
matters sexual. Slightly more than fifty years after De Eruditione Dante was to provide a wholly different hierarchy of sins
in which those related to sexuality were less heinous than the
colder and more calculated of crimes.[3]

Vincent combines age with gender, for it is in the youth of a woman that temptation is at its greatest, "in etate que prona est lascivie."[4] To combat this possible wantonness the girls should be physically controlled. It is most important to notice in gauging Vincent's response to traditional attitudes that he is at pains to qualify the restrictions on girls attending dances, plays and social gatherings. The limitations of spectacula (plays) might make him seem as stern as Tertullian who in his De Spectaculis thought plays should be completely forbidden, viewing the Last Judgment as the only spectacle worth considering and who had some consistently negative comments regarding plays:

> Omne enim spectaculum sine concussione spiritus non est. Ubi enim voluptas, ibi est studium, per quod scilicet voluptas sapit; ubi studium, ibi et aemulatio, per quam studium sapit. Porro et ubi aemulatio, ibi et furor et bilis et ira et dolor et cetera ex his, quae cum his non competunt disciplinae.[5]

But this is not so. Vincent adds "non passim", key phrase of temperance and moderation. It is not total prohibition, but limitation that Vincent is urging. This moderation of the outright prohibition is precisely that which marks off Vincent's view from those of his eminent predecessors throughout De Eruditione.

This healthy concept of moderation does not, however, prevent Vincent from agreeing fully with the idea that the body of a daughter must be guarded chiefly so as to avoid parental embarrassment, "parentibus . . . opprobrium." He also seems to hold that girls are responsible for their own lusts and also the lusts in others, "ne vagantes concupiscant vel concupiscantur." This doubling of responsibility heightens the need for the proper education a girl is to receive. It seems that Vincent is rather more concerned with the effect on others, i.e. parents, husbands, men in general, than he is with the effect upon the girl herself. For him there is a foregone conclusion to the question 'Who sins most, the tempter or the tempted'-- girls are both. In this attitude he is a true son of both Jerome and Aristotle; and whatever praise Vincent earns for his partially enlightened views, we must conclude that he is scarcely better than his brother Dominican and fellow Aristotelian, Thomas Aquinas, who wrote:

> Sicut enim Philosophus dicit in XVI De Animalibus, mulier est vir occasionatus.[6]

Vincent also accepts the curious physiology of earlier times which provides a physical punishment for moral transgressions. Although in general it is Vincent's practice to stress the educational advantages of praise rather than blame, reward rather than punishment, he does admit that a woman can effect her own barrenness, "vel per nimiam concubitus frequentacionem." It is a significant omission on the part of Vincent who played a vital role in the transmission of Aristotle's biology and who was living at the very time when "the free experimental study of medicine which had characterized the school of Salerno was replaced by an authoritarianism glorifying Galen,"[7] that he failed to cite the Galenic obverse to this fantasy, to wit that intercourse on the part of man diminishes his life by a day.[8]

An important presupposition in Vincent's system of argument

by appeal to scriptural authority is that in part at least the
Old Testament is not only in a pre-figurative way influential
in the New Testament and thus upon the present, but it is lit-
erally and legally binding in the present, (regarding adultery) "sibi quoque legem mortis iudicium." For what law could
this be?--surely not the Regulae of Ulpian who for all the restrictions on the Roman matron's weakness as revealed in "Mutus,
surdus, furiosus, pupillus femina neque familiae emptor esse
neque testis libripensue fieri potest"[9] did say "nuptias non
concubitus, sed consensus facit."[10] Nor is it clearly to
Deuteronomy that Vincent is appealing. There was a tradition
that the Christian dispensation abrogated the old law, but
Vincent seems to deny that the old law is ever in any way al-
tered by Christ as he quotes from the text that underscores
and expatiates upon the old Mosaic code in details which make
Hammurabi and Draco seem clement: thus Deuteronomy XXII, 20,
21:

> Quod si verum est quod objicit, et non est puella inventa
> virginitas, ejicient eam extra fores domus patris sui, et
> lapidibus obruent viri civitatis illius, et morietur,
> quoniam fecit nefas in Israel, ut fornicaretur in domo
> patris sui, et auferes malum de medio tue.[11]

When one has solved this question of what law, one turns
the page only to find that Vincent himself tells us that it is
indeed Deuteronomy. This practice of repetitive citation may be
equally a rhetorical use of the device repetition or an indication of haste in composition. It is the considered judgment here
that the former is the case, for throughout his writings Vincent
holds to the view that we need not so much to be instructed as

reminded.

In the midst of all this offensive stress on parental and familial shame caused by filial transgression, Vincent shows still that he is aware of the extremity to which the early authors so often went and the consequent requirement of qualification. Thus he is careful to insist upon the age factor rather than any personal shortcoming when he provides the parenthetical comment, "id est ad luxuriam propter etatis fervorem pronam."[12] It is in these brief but telling parenthetical modifications, together with the particular hierarchy of citations, that the original contribution of Vincent lies. These qualifiers must be sought in the midst of odd turnings of reference, as in this opening chapter, where the focus is first on the girl, then on the male members of the family. Thus in quoting Jerome in order to support his contention that youth is a time requiring the utmost watchfulness, "tenera res est in feminis pudicicie fama, quasi flos . . . ad levem cito marescit auram . . . maxime, ubi consentit etas et maritalis deest auctoritas, cuius umbra tutamen uxoris est."[13] What Vincent has done has been to expatiate upon the wide-ranging effects of youthful wantonness, effects which he forgets about as he returns to the application of his argument that the girl avoid lust lest she "aliqua occasione sibi atque causam infamie prestet."[14]

The next parenthetical modification by Vincent underlines just how basically the education of girls is to be moral rather than intellectual. Quoting Ecclesiasticus on the foolish daughter, he glosses 'fatua' as 'indisciplinata et dissoluta.' Here

Vincent shifts from the intellectual sphere to the moral, for
the weakness here is suggested by the word 'fatua.' For the
usual synonyms in Classical Latin and approved by Isidore are
'stupidus', 'herbes', 'ineptus', 'insulsus', 'absurdus'--
all of which have the meanings 'foolish', 'silly', or 'simple'. Perhaps such as are 'fatuae' are so simple as to be
undisciplined in the way a simpleton is, but that very sim-
ple-mindedness makes them less culpable of dissoluteness unless, that is, one cares to stretch the bonds of language to
the breaking point. Vincent is willing to do so in order to
stress completely the supremacy of moral education in his treatise.

If he does not scruple to bend words, he is certainly not
hesitant to juggle scripture. Immediately following his remark
about the foolish daughter, as is his wont, he supplies an illustration. Usually he has positive examples, but here he has
the negative one of Dinah in Genesis 34, a negative example he
repeats in quotation from Jerome's letter to Laeta at the close
of the opening chapter. Just how biased a point of view Vincent's is can be seen by the fact that he chooses to recall only a part of the story that favors his position and repress that
part of it which does not.

Few who have read the story of innocent and oddly loved
Dinah will forget that it appears in the midst of the most ob-
scenely barbarous section of the entire Old Testament. The
Bible makes perfectly clear that Dinah was forced against her
will and that afterwards her lover, regretful of his act and

full of love for her, sought her in marriage:

> Egressa est autem Dina filia liae, ut videret mulieres
> regionis illius. Quam cum vidisset Sichem filius Hemor
> hevaei, princeps, terrae illius, adamavit eam, ut rapuit,
> et dormivit cum illa, vi opprimens virginem. Et conglu-
> tinata est anima eius cum ea, tristemque delinivit bland-
> ditiis. Et pergens ad puellam hanc coniugen.[15]

Now not only does Vincent omit the consequent turpitude of her

brothers, the sons of Jacob, but also the duplicity perpetrated

by Laban upon Jacob and Jacob's willingness to smooth over the

offense in regard to Dinah's own conception--all celebrated and

infamous Old Testament events, but he goes on to say that Dinah

is "de qua legitur in Proverb VII:--Talis est mulier garrula et

vaga, quietis impaciens, nec valens in domo consistere pedibus

suis, sed nunc foris, nunc in plateis, nunc iuxta angulos in-

sidians."[16] Here Vincent, in his zeal for analogies to support

his position, jumps right across the age distinction he had been

at pains to stress earlier, for no writer of Latin ever thought

puella (word used in Genesis) and mulier (word used in Proverbs)

were synonyms. Further he glosses over completely the fact of

Dinah's innocence which even the Draconian Deuteronomy allowed

for in the midst of its penalties. Below the section cited by

Vincent earlier in the chapter we find:

> Sin autem in agro repererit vir puellam, quae desponsata est,
> et apprehendens concubuerit cum ea, ipse morietur solus; puella
> nihil patietur, nec est rea mortis . . . Si invenerit vir
> puellam virginem, quae non habet sponsum, et apprehendens
> concubuerit cum illa, et res iudicium venerit, dabit qui dor-
> mivit cum ea, patri puellae quinquaginta siclos argenti, et
> habebit eam uxorem, quia humiliavit illam; non poterit dimittere
> eam cunctis diebus vitae suae.[17]

Vincent having omitted these significant references, goes

on to cite Jerome in one of his choicer satirical morsels drawn

from a rather unholy personal and exact knowledge. In all the
performance is a quite oddly and inexactly illustrated argument
for the watching of daughters.

To understand still further the fact that this educator of
girls is primarily moral rather than intellectual, we should note
that Vincent offers the Blessed Virgin Mary as a counter moral
example to the invidious Dinah. The entire stress is on the
well-protected rearing of Mary, with no reference whatsoever to
her intellectual attainments. This omission is a striking manifestation of Vincent's limited focus, for at about the very time
that Vincent of Beauvais was penning these moral exempla, Albertus Magnus in his Mariale asked two hundred and thirty questions relating to the Annunciation.

The answer to question ninety has the following: Did the
Blessed Virgin Mary possess a perfect knowledge of the seven
liberal arts? "It seems to me that she did . . . for it is written, 'Wisdom hath built herself a house, she hath hewn her out
seven pillars' Prov. IX.1) This house is the Blessed Virgin;
the seven pillars are the seven liberal arts. Mary was then
endowed with a perfect knowledge of them."[18] Albert goes on to
gloss Exodus 111.22 "sed postulabit mulier a vicina sua, et ab
hospita sua vasa argentea et aures" as a request for knowledge
of the earthly sciences, sciences known by both the Saints and
the Blessed Virgin Mary; and even more ingeniously Canticle of
Canticles IV, 4: "Sicut turris David collum tuum quae aedificata
est cum propugnaculis: mille clypei pendent ex ea, omnis arma-
tura" as 'the tower of David is the Holy Scripture, the bucklers

are the natural sciences; but the liberal arts are the arsenal
of the Scriptures, and it belongs to the Saints to know them.
The same privilege, therefore, is due to the Mother of God."[19]
With this interpretation of the Blessed Virgin Mary's intellectual virtues in addition to the moral and theological, one can
see how, if Mary is to serve as a model, one easily can make her
intellectually exemplary. But Vincent does not choose to use
her so, satisfying himself with Ambrosian references to her
flight from publicity.

Sara, though not so 'apocryphal' as Mary, is quite with-
drawn from society, especially was it: "numquam cum ludentibus
miscui me."[20] In Vincent's educational plan, play does have a
small role as is clear from the references to the education of
small children in the Speculum Doctrinale where an hour of play
is allotted to the young child both before and after breakfast.
Yet in the chapters devoted specifically to the education of
girls Vincent seems to avoid mention of play, while at the same
time invoking at every opportunity references and authorites to
support an attack on laziness and to advance the cause of work.
Truly for Vincent, idle hands are the devil's workshop.

Such play as there was, was for the time of childhood and
"in any case the early marriages of the day meant short childhood."[21] So that given the long range moral goals Vincent was
allotting only the just amount of leisure. Further he seems to
have been generally a devotee of work, so much so that he is
viewed by so distinquished a scholar as Emile Mâle who has cited
Vincent's Speculum Doctrinale as an important vehicle for the

promulgation of the idea called the "beatification of manual labor."[22] Of course his own prodigious labors made him a model
of the theory he preached. Yet one misses just a little the
view of the Menagier of Paris, who began to devote the third and
last part of his little treatise to the _amusements_ proper to his
young wife's leisure hours.[23] Further still we may note at how
great distance Vincent with his insistence on filling up the day
with profitable work was from St. Thomas and his belief in the
cultural necessity of leisure. "Compared with the exclusive i-
dea of work as activity, leisure implies (in the first place) an
attitude of non-activity, of inward calm, or silence; it means
not being 'busy,' but letting things happen. Leisure is a form
of silence . . . for leisure is a receptive attitude of mind,
a contemplative attitude . . ."[24] Of course, Vincent was not
a philosopher and if forced into a discussion of the vexed question, and particularly vexed for the Dominican and Pope of the
relative relation of act and contemplation, he may well have
come closer to the Thomistic position, but as he was not, we can
notice only his great use of work, the better to avoid both leisure and the devil.

Vincent concludes his negative, defensive, and minatory
opening chapter on the education of girls with a rhetorical
question culled from St. Jerome to the effect that abstinence
from danger is safer than a tempting of danger by juxtaposition.
The company one keeps is all important, rather oddly not for the
possible harm the nearness of such evil persons may have on the
morals of the girls, but for the effect on her reputation. De-

traction will not allow her virtue, "libidinosa mens ardencius honesta prosequitur et quod non licet, dulcius suspicatur."[25] From that strange note we move to the most important of the chapters for the intellectual training of girls.

As with boys, the girls are to be instructed in both letters and morals. Perhaps because it is a similar education in letters and a dissimilar one in morals that so much of the stress of the chapter is on the moral aspect and so much of the education in letters has already been discussed in the earlier chapters, especially 2-13. Throughout this chapter, as indeed throughout the entire treatise, Vincent's attitude is quite Christian and very non-Grecian; that is, he has no confidence that the greater the intellectual understanding therefore the better the person, or, as is sometimes said, knowledge is virtue. Quite the contrary, there are times when Vincent is almost totally concerned with moral training independent of intellectual study. Thus, even when, as in this chapter, he is concerned with the activity of the mind, he makes it a handmaiden rather than a cause of virtue.

His first judgment in the chapter is based on Chrysostom's fear of leisure to the effect that reading is a time-filler designed to ward off idle and possible lustful thought. He cites Jerome in the same way: girls should read and learn as much as possible to the point of falling asleep over the scred text. This seems a bit extreme, but then in history there is the counter example of Francesca da Rimini[26] who did not read enough. Also from Jerome, Vincent approves of a first acquaintance with

letters through religious poetry, i.e. Psalms, that her first
wrestlings with the alphabet be aided by wooden and ivory blocks
the names of which she is to cite, that play itself be a vehicle
of education, "lusus eius eruditio sit," and that competition
among her peers be introduced with the reward of praise (this is
a principle used later by the Jesuits--and the dangers to pride
which even among girls was recognized by St. Thomas More.)[27]
Nowhere more clearly than in this selection from St. Jerome do
we learn so much about Vincent's theories from his habit of
patchwork quotations. The penultimate sentence (as those above
it) is taken from section four of Jerome's letter to Laeta; but
the last sentence dealing with the need for a girl to focus on
the correctness of the text's transcription rather upon any il-
lumination is taken from section twelve. There is no indication
to the reader as to the material omitted--and the omission is of
the utmost importance.

The first omission is that of the 'magister' who is to be
chosen as tutor to the noble virgin. It may well be that the
oversight is explained by the fact that the education of the
boys and girls is to be the same up to a certain point in age
and that thus the comments made regarding the qualities of a
teacher in Chapters Two and Three are to be applied equally
here. If so, then one notices that both Jerome and Vincent are
arguing for a male instructor for female students. It would be
a great help towards our understanding of Vincent's true educational theory if we knew at precisely what age the instruction
of the boys and girls was no longer to be the same. He says only

"Porro quod dictum est supra de pueris, idem quoque agendum est is etate tenera de puellis . . ."[28]  Certainly it could not remain the same at puberty, for then Vincent would be defying Jerome's admonition, "Procul sit aetas lasciva puerorum."[29]  But whether it was only at puberty or at some time before remains a moot point.  What is clear is that the girls are taught by a man, but a man significantly "probae aetatis."[30]

The character and skills of the teacher are spelled out in some detail by Vincent who bases much on the exemplary force of the teacher himself in support of his precepts, "et revera vite honestas et maturitas in doctore auctoritatem adquirit et multum in auditoribus proficit."[31]  What he does not stress is the role of the mother in the early education of children--a significant omission considering that it was a woman who had commissioned the work, and as we have elsewhere pointed out his selections are from works which do mention the educational role of mothers.  Just as Vincent in drawing from Suetonius makes no mention of the role of Atia in the growth of Augustus, here he omits from Jerome's Letter to Laeta the reference to even more celebrated "Gracchorum eloquentiae multum ab infantia sermo matris scribitur contulisse . . ."[32]

In dealing with the necessary skills of the teacher Vincent does raise an issue which is important in primary education, but which was even more a matter of contention on the university level, that is, the question of the rate at which the teacher should deliver his instructions.  One can easily appreciate the need for a teacher's not speaking too rapidly, especially as the pupils might not yet be masters of the stylus and parchment. Yet it is not just the rapidity that Vincent is anxious to slow down but also the reverse: "Observanda est eciam in docendo maturitas, i.e. inter velocitatem et tarditatem mediocritas, ut enim, seneca dicit lucilium: 'inopia verborum et exilitas minus intentum auditorem facit, interrupte tedio tarditatis facilius tamen insidet, quod expectatur, quam quod pretervolat' . . . Itaque cavenda est et nimia inculcacio et eciam nimia interrupcio."[33] This awareness that interruptions do refrigerate the mind and that too slow a lecture cannot hold the attention show Vincent had some insights in the matter of the psychology of learning. In the larger world of higher education the same problem was solved in a striking way by statute at the University of Paris:

> Two methods of lecturing on books in the liberal arts
> having been tried, the former masters of philosophy
> uttering their words rapidly so that the mind of
> the hearer can take them in but the hand cannot keep
> up with them, the latter speaking slowly until their
> listeners can catch up with them with the pen; hav-
> ing compared these by diligent examination, the for-
> mer method is found the better . . . therefore . . .
> all lecturers . . . wherever and whenever they chance
> to lecture on any text ordinarily or cursorily . . .
> shall observe the former method of lecturing to the
> best of their ability, so speaking forsooth as if no
> one was taking notes before them, in the way that ser-
> mons and recommendations are made in the university
> and which the lectures in other faculties follow.[34]

Whatever their historical limitations it is clear that at times Vincent and other mediaeval educators were coming to terms with problems whose interest and importance are felt just as deeply now as then.

The second chief omission occurs in section 9 of Jerome's letter:

> Reddat tibi pensum cotidie scripturam certum. Ediscat
> Graecorum versuum numerum. Sequatur statim et Latina
> eruditio; quae si non ab initio os tenerum composuit,
> in peregrinum sonum lingua corrumpitur et externis
> vitiis sermo patruus sordidatur.[35]

The issue of language is a vital one in understanding Vincent of
Beauvais' educational views. In what language was instruction
carried on at the court tutorials? Latin presumably, and not
French. And in what language were the texts which were studied?
Latin presumably, and not Greek. To take the second first following the order of Jerome, we may say that the question of the
knowledge of Greek in the Middle Ages is a vexed one. We know
that Jerome learned it and that Augustine did not, to his great
chagrin. We know that the issue of whether or not Latin or
Greek was the language spoken by Cassiodorus and his fellow
monks[36] at Vivarium in the middle of vestigial Magna Graecia has
been settled in favor of Latin (and the poor monks who did know
Greek were terribly overworked as a result). We are aware that
the notion of preservation of a Greek tradition by the Irish
monks must be viewed with some qualifying skepticiam and that
even Thomas Aquinas needed William of Moerbeke to translate Aristotle for him[37] and that in general we may say, that up to and
continuing through the time of Vincent, Greek was not a language
seriously and sufficiently studied. Vincent's own citations of
Greek writers are always made from Latin translations. So much
for "graecorum versum numerum." But what of "sermo patruus?"
Vincent and the Capetians could scarcely have felt that Frankish
Latin was a pure strain of Latin that must be protected from
foreign influences. The Franks were themselves those foreigners.

Yet at this very time there was a growth of feeling that can in
later days be called nationalism as a consciousness of one's
own tongue--not Latin, but a vernacular language, in this case
French.  It is an open question as to the degree of French usage.
We know only that the vernacular had somewhat of a bad reputation in that many heresies began by being transmitted in the
vernacular[38] and those writings not heretical in the vernacular
were trivial and thus designed for the minds of women, or so
some say.  We recall that Juvenal said that women were particularly open to the enthusiasm for heresy.  On the other side of
the coin is the fact that French was the first vernacular to
arise and the first to blossom.  Even Vincent, unless there was
a Dominican Alcuin at his shoulder querying "Quid enim _Rolandus_
cum Christo?", could not have been ignorant of the fact that

> all this imaginative literature, _chansons de geste_, _chansons
> courtoises_, verse and prose romances, which was read or
> heard from one end of Europe to the other, is marked by two
> essential characteristics; it is based upon religious sen-
> timent and belief, and the ideal upheld is that of the
> kinghtly virutes.[39]

The next great encyclopaedist after Vincent himself wrote his
_Tresor_ in French (though he himself was what we might call an
Italian) "for the reason that in his opinion 'La Parleure fran-
caise est plus delitable et plus commune a toutes gens.'"[40]  Of
course as Vincent says, "Sicut enim deus est finis omnium rerum,
sic et theologica scientia, que est de divinis, est finis omnium
arcium."[41]  "For theological or what might be called scientific
purposes, Latin naturally came first; it was generally known,
and it possessed the vocabulary required for dealing with tech-

nical subjects, to a degree which no vernacular could claim."[42]

Vincent seems to have considered other languages besides Latin,
for one of the suggested tasks of the more advanced students is
to "peregrine lingue scripturas interpretando vel eciam exponen-
do."[43] Translation, but of what "peregrine lingue?" It is not
Greek; but if not Greek, then Hebrew? Scarcely, as the state of
western Hebraic studies was almost nonexistent at the time. Then
it is a vernacular, including French, for Vincent with Latin as
his daily vehicle of expression would find even French "peregrine." Vincent could thus assume a reading knowledge of at
least French literature among his Latiners. It still remains
one of the alluring mysteries of Vincent's pedagogy that his method of teaching Latin may or may not have been more or less
direct. We know how Montaigne learned Latin directly:

> And so, without any arificial means, without any book, with-
> out grammar or teaching, without any rod and without tears,
> I learned a Latin quite as pure as that of my schoolmaster.[44]

and how Plutarch moved from Greek to Latin.

> In the reading of Latin books, singular as it may appear,
> I did not find that the words assisted me to discover
> the meaning but rather that my knowledge of the history
> enabled me to find out the meaning of the words.[45]

We know Vincent could not have used a perfectly direct method,
for he says: "Itaque scienciarum omnium gramatica est fundamen-
tum, quam hodie multi tamquam vilem negligunt et ideo parum in
aliis proficere possunt."[46]

The books acceptable for reading by the students are not
cited individually by title so that there is no help regarding
a correct understanding of the possible role of vernacular texts.

Whether this is the door opening on to the road of vernacular
study, given the number of texts in French espousing one kind
of heresy or another, is not clear.  Vincent lived and wrote at
the very moment when the vernacular languages, particularly
French, were coming into their own.  On the value of them and of
their use in education he is, alas, remarkably silent.

The third omission occurs just after the reference to the
manuscripts of the Holy Scripture.  Jerome proceeds to provide
a detailed ordering of the Bible readings.  There is nothing
like it in Vincent.  We know that he is a bit skeptical about
the value of secular poetry:

> At quid enim usque hodie parvulorum sensus et lingue poeticis
> fabulis ac luxuriosis figmentis imbuuntur?  Nam et in doctrina
> poetica sit utilis quantum ad regulas metricas, inutilis tam
> est, immo perniciosa quantum ad fabulas predictas.[47]

He supports this contention by citing Augustine, although not
the one who thought we should spoil the Egyptians, but the
younger Augustine who wept for Dido but not for his own sins.
Skeptical of that as he may be, he seems equally skeptical of
the value of the Old Testament, for in his list of acceptable
readings (not structured as in Jerome) he avoids it entirely,
and thus is spared the difficulty of the Song of Songs, which
Jerome squarely confronts:

> Discat primum Psalterium, his se canticis avocet, et
> in Proverbiis Salomoniis erudiatur ad vitam . . . Cumque
> pectoris sui cellarium his opibus locupletarit, mandet
> memoriae Prophetus et Heptateuchum et Regum ac Para-
> lipomenon libros Hesdraeque et Hester volumina, ut
> ultimum sine periculo discat Canticum Canticorum, ne,
> si in exordio legerit, sub carnalibus verbis spiritua-
> lium nuptiarum epithalamium non intellegemus vulneretur.[48]

Although Vincent practices allegorical reading and doubtless

approved of it as an interpretive tool, it seems here that he
is avoiding the one flagrantly clear case of its need. We learn
almost as much about Vincent from what he wilfully omits as we
do from what he says.

Indeed, to return to what Vincent next says in his own text,
he approvingly quotes Jerome: "rubrum huius seculi pelagus
transfretare", the full meaning of which can best be understood
only by use of allegorical interpretation, as we have elsewhere
stated.

Reading, of course, is only part of Vincent's curriculum,
and it is by no means the most important. Indeed, by virtue of
its limited role, its nature must be more precisely delineated.
A girl's education must be composed of "oracio et operacio"[49]
in addition to her reading which is already primarily if not
totally scriptural. Prayer is viewed less as a vehicle to bring
a girl closer to God than to protect her from temptation, "solet
huiuscemodi clipeo repellantur."[50] Action is important also as
a defensive tactic against idleness and the devil. Thus handicrafts are not so much valuable in themselves as "ut per occa-
sionem operis nihil aliud cogites nisi quod ad domini pertinet
servitutem."[51] It is important to notice that this function of
physical action is not restricted to the education of girls, for
Vincent specifically quotes Jerome in his epistle to Rusticum,
"quod tam feminis quam viris est necessarium."[52]

Of some significance for a proto-humanist awareness of the
importance of notebooks is the exemplum drawn from Suetonius,
the limitation of which has been cited above: "et quod in

diuturnos vel diurnas referretur commentarios vetaret."[53] However Vincent does not elaborate on the value of this practice,
preferring to return to his basic theme that reading is but a
part of the triptych of reading, praying and working.

As an interlude in the midst of reading and praying and
working, Vincent approves the idea of Jerome that a girl "hymnos
decantet"[54]--a limited but cited aspect of musical education.
While there is a great gap between 'musike' as understood by
Plato and other Greek thinkers and music as offered by Jerome
and Vincent, it is nonetheless an aspect of Vincent's tuition
for girls that should not be forgotten, especially inasmuch as
Vincent's general attitude toward elements that can be considered as play is quite negative.

Quite specifically Vincent says that the education of girls
is the same as that for boys at this particular age. Yet he
never specifically defines "in etate tenera," an omission that
seriously limits the confidence with which an historian can correctly understand his pedagogy. Whatever the age at which the
genders are separated, before that division they are both instructed "in moribus et consuetudinibus bonis"--a distinction
between theory and practice, a distinction underscored by the
following dichotomy between work and deed, "quorum alterum lingue,
alterum moribus officiat."[55] One is accustomed to reading religious, and particularly Catholic, writers who use a trichotomous
division of morality into thought, work and deed. While there
is no  suggestion that Vincent ignored the importance of thought
as either good or evil, it is true that in De Eruditione he

focused entirely on the observable aspects of morality: word and deed.

Having just stated that moral instruction and good habits are his educational goals, Vincent then states that the first four of these goals are "sc. in pudicicia sine castitate et in humilitate et in taciturnitate et in morum sive gestum maturitate."[56] If pride of place is assigned to the first, then, as the context of the work supports, chastity is the most important of these four. Vincent approves the idea of Cyprian that chastity and prudence is not only part and parcel of Vincent's view of the near perfect identification of sexual purity and the whole of moral virtue, but it is an anticipation of Thomism. For, if one understands chastity in the larger sense, as Origen (quoted immediately after Cyprian) seems to hold, as a discipline leading to virtue, one sees how closely its role approximates that of prudence as held by St. Thomas Aquinas. One needs scarcely remind the attentive reader that however close chastity and prudence may be, the distinction that has only men possessed with prudence is a serious and near-damning limitation on the intellectual capacity of women as judged by Vincent of Beauvais. For Thomas prudence is not that narrow, pragmatically defensive quality one sees every day in the successful accountant or cautious student who avoids the tougher courses in the interest of higher grades. It is the _first_ of the four cardinal virtues, indeed the one without which temperance, fortitude and justice are not virutes at all, "omnis virtus moralis debet esse prudens."[57] "Prudentia dicitur genetrix virtutum." On the basis in Thomism that the truth must precede goodness we may accept: "What is prudent and what is good are substantially one and the same; they differ only in their place in the logical succession of realization. For whatever is good must first have been prudent."[58] Given this view of prudence as the sine qua non of virtue, one is able to note that Vincent keeps the idea of central importance for chastity, but he diminishes the aspect of intellectual awareness.

The two enemies against which chastity is to be the most active are "maximaque a carnis delectacione superflua et a societate mala."[59] The former has five subdivisions "a delectacione, inquam, superflua in cibo et potu et somno et balneo et ornatu."[60] The ascetic Jerome is invoked in a gamut length citation of the sensual temptations possible to eye, ear, tongue, hand and nostrils--with a great stress on tongue and hand. A full stomach and a freshly bathed body seem together to be the most dangerous state for a girl. Jerome does not appear to have been an enthusiast of clean linen. His fasts and abstinence are well known. The valuable theme to be elicited from all of this asceticism is that of Vincent's acceptance of extreme abstinence as the source of some virtues. He takes this directly from Jerome in Contra Joviniarum. He could have gone to Jerome's Epitaphium Sanctae Paulae where at the conclusion of the rehearsal of the rigid regimen Paula imposed upon herself, St. Jerome utilizes his knowledge of the Greek philosophers when he mentions that, difficult though it may be to avoid the extremes, the philosophers are quite right in their opinion that virtue

is a mean and vice an excess, or as we may express it in one
short phrase, "ne quid nimis." There are always internal tensions in the heart of intellectual liberals who have a cordial
conservatism. As Jerome himself had elsewhere pointed out
"where your treasure is there is your heart also." None of the
Fathers is quite so inconsistent and self-contradictory as Jerome. It is thus of some significance that, from among these
tensions, Vincent draws upon only those which surround the pole
of ascetic extremism rather than that of classical golden mediocritas.

After drawing upon Ovid as an authority for the argument
that prosperity is a danger and the obverse a safeguard: "Ve-
neris dampnosa libido non solet in mestos sepe venire thoros,"[61]
Vincent returns to Jerome again for citations concerning the
need to avoid food and drink by means of fasting: "melius est
stomachum quam mentem te dolere imperare corpori quam servire,
gressus quam pudiciciam vacillare" and "sic comedat, ut semper
esuriat et statim post cibum orare ac legere valeat."[62] There
is a good deal of extreme rigor in the first quotation and some
latent in the idea of forever keeping an edge of hunger in the
second, and Vincent quickly points out that Jerome was aware of
the need of moderation lest "debilitatur corpus viribus."[63] Thus
"Michi disciplicent in teneris etatibus maxime longa et immo-
derata ieiunia."[64] Jerome, not Vincent, spells out the limits
of 'teneris etatibus,' an omission which is a serious limitation on our ability to determine exactly the gradations in the
Vincentian pedagogy. Of course, Jerome may well have been

thinking of those women who not only mortified the flesh by
fasting too much, but in the process so enlarged their self-
confidence that they became insane. "After living in cold,
damp cells they do not know where they are, where they are going or what they are saying . . . he complains that such women
begin to think they know something about Scriptures; they cannot keep their mouths shut; they insist on lecturing about biblical passages of which they understand nothing; and finally
they adopt airs of scholars."[65] It will be remembered that Jerome's humanism stops short of educating women in the classics.
Here one sees how he puts a ceiling to the amount of sacred
knowledge they may be expected to demonstrate. Vincent, to the
degree that he draws upon Jerome's view on female learning, can
scarcely be called humanistic. And, of course, in the midst of
all this Vincent can convey a seeming humanism by citing Terence
from the _Eunuchus_, appropriately enough: "Sine cerere et baccho
friget venus."[66] Now Terence was admired for the purity of his
Latinity and perhaps for the conclusion of his plays which however much immorality is displayed within the works, the resolu-
tion lies in the respectability of marriage. Further still of
course Jerome's own teacher Donatus has a celebrated commentary
on Terence. The fact remains however that this veneer of classicism comes from the _collectanea_ and is but the mediaeval ic-
ing to a stale cake of ascetic elements.

Having focused on food and drink, Vincent moves to sleep
and baths and in so doing opens the door to _education_ _at_ _night_
in quoting Jerome: "Filia tua nocte ad oraciones surgat, mane

hymnos decantet et oracioni lectio . . . succedat."[67] The chapter concludes on a note which shows how far from Sparta and Plato Jerome's, and by implication Vincent's, view of female education is. What does Athens have to do with Jerusalem indeed--
no need for the strigil, the oil, the sponge here. No need for
any Phidias or Praxiteles, no Aphrodite of Knidos or the Aphrodite by Doedalsas.

[1]"You have sons?  Train them and care for them from boyhood.  You have daughters?  Watch over their bodies and do not show yourself joyful to them."

[2]See the New Catholic Edition of the Holy Bible  (New York: Catholic Book Publishing Company, 1953), p. 743.

[3]Dante, Inferno, Dorothy L. Sayers, trans. (New York: Penguin Books, 1964), p. 140.

[4]"at the age which has a tendency for lust."

[5]"For no public entertainment is lacking in danger to the spirit.  For where there is pleasure, there is zeal which pleasure savors; where there is zeal, there is rivalry which adds spice to zeal.  And where there is rivalry, there is anger and wrath and rage and pain and all the other things which stem from them and which along with them are not  appropriate to discipline of the spirit."

[6]"A woman is a mutilated man."

[7]R. R. Bolgar, The Classical Heritage and its Beneficiaries (New York: Harper and Row, 1954), p. 235.

[8]John Donne Complete Poetry, John Hayward, ed. (London: The Nonesuch Library, 1955), p. 53, "Farewell to Love."

[9]"Neither a mute nor deaf person nor madman nor orphan nor woman nor purchaser for a family can become either a witness or a paymaster."

[10]"A marriage is made by consensus not cohabitation."

[11]"But if it happens that there is no virginity, they will throw the girl outside her father's house and the men will stone

her and she will die since she has done evil to Israel to sin in her father's house and you will put this evil from your midst."

[12]"i.e. that she has a tendency to enjoyment because of the passion of her age."

[13]"the reputation for chastity is an ephemeral thing in women . . . like a flower . . . it begins to decay in a light wind . . . particularly when the age is a factor and the authority of the husband is lacking, the husband whose shadow is the safety of his wife."

[14]"On some occasion she would present the opportunity for disgrace."

[15]"But Dinah, daughter of Lia, went out to see the women of her region. When Sichem, son of Hemor, prince of the region, had seen her, he took her and slept with her by force. He became attached to her and spoke tenderly to her. Going to his father, Hemor, he said, get that girl for me for my wife."

[16]"Such is the woman, talkative and roaming, unable to be quiet, unable to stay at home, but now outside, now in the squares, now lying in wait in the corners."

[17]"If a man finds a betrothed girl in a field, seizes her and seduces her, he alone will die: the girl is not to blame nor is it a capital offense . . . if a man comes upon a virgin who is not betrothed, seizes her and it is discovered, he will pay her father fifty silver pieces and marry her because he disgraced her; nor can he send her away all the days of her life."

[18]J. Sighart, Albert the Great (London: Washbourne, 1976), p. 331.

[19]Sighart, p. 332.

[20]"I have never joined in play."

[21]Eileen Power in The Legacy of the Middle Ages, edited by Crum and Jacob (Oxford: University Press, 1926), p. 420.

[22]G. R. Owst, _Literature and Pulpit in Medieval England_ (New York: Barnes and Noble, 1933), p. 568.

[23]Eileen Power, p. 430.

[24]Joseph Pieper, _Prudence_ (New York: Pantheon Books, 1959), p. 52.

[25]"A lustful mind approaches honorable things more eagerly and what is not permitted is undertaken more sweetly."

[26]Dorothy Sayers, pp. 100-101.

[27]_St. Thomas More: Selected Letters_, Elizabeth Frances Rogers, ed. (New Haven: Yale Press, 1961), p. 106.

[28]"What has been said before about boys, the same must be done at the tender age for girls."

[29]"Let the lustful age of boys be far away."

[30]"of upright age."

[31]"An upright life, honesty and maturity in the teacher brings authority and accomplishes much in the learners."

[32]"It is written that the speech of the mother in their infancy contributed much to the eloquence of the Gracchi."

[33]"Maturity in teaching must be looked for i.e. moderation between speed and slowness. For as Seneca said to Lucilius: scarcity of words and thinness make the listener less intent: the tedium of slowness fixes itself more easily, what is expected rather than what flies by. And so one must beware too much inculcating and too much interruption."

[34]D. W. Sylvester, _Educational Documents 800-1816_ (London: Methuen and Co., 1970), p. 70.

[35]"Let her daily repeat to you a fixed part of Scriptures. Let her learn a number of Greek verses. Let learning of Latin follow close after. If the tender lips do not learn from the beginning, the language is corrupted to a foreign accent and our native speech is debased by alien faults." See Quintilian on the order to be observed in learning Greek and Latin.

[36]Pierre Courcelle, Late Latin Writers and Their Greek Sources, Harry E. Wedeck, trans. (Cambridge: Harvard Press, 1969), p. 338.

[37]L. J. Paetow, Guide to the Study of Medieval History (Berkeley: University of California Press, 1917), p. 396.

[38]Joan Evans, Life in Medieval France (New York: Phaidon, 1957), p. 47.

[39]H. J. Chaytor, From Script to Print (New York: October House, 1966), p. 3.

[40]Chaytor, p. 23.

[41]"For thus God is the end of all things, and thus theology which concerns the divine, is the end of all arts."

[42]Chaytor, p. 23.

[43]"by interpreting and explaining scripture in a foreign language."

[44]The Essays of Montaigne trans. by E. J. Trechman (London: Oxford Press), Vol. I, p. 174.

[45]Ibid.

[46]"And so grammar is the basis of all knowledge, which too many neglect as worthless and can accomplish too little in others."

[47]"And why should the senses be daily filled with stories of the poets and wild imaginings? For let there be something useful in poetry concerning metrics, for nothing is useless even in the dangerous words of the poets."

[48]"Let her learn first the Psalter and let her take some time off with these songs and let her learn of life in Proverbs of Solomon . . . when she has made the storehouse of her mind rich with these pleasures, let her commit to memory Prophets, Heptateuch, book of Kings and Chronicles, and rolls of Ezra and Esther so that finally she may read the Song of Songs without danger. If she read it at the start, she might be harmed by not realizing that it was a wedding song expressed in carnal language."

[49]"Prayer and Action."

[50]"They are repelled by a shield of this kind."

[51]"So that through the opportunity of work you may think of nothing else but what pertains to the service of the Lord."

[52]"necessary for men as well as women."

[53]"in order that he might prevent their doing anything that could not be noted in daily notebooks or longer journals."

[54]"Let her sing songs."

[55]"Harm on the one hand in work, on the other in deed."

[56]"In purity and chastity and humility and silence and maturity of behavior and morals."

[57]"All moral virtue ought to be prudent."

[58]Pieper, p. 19.

[59]"especially from excessive pleasures of the flesh and bad associations."

[60]"From excessive delight in food, drink, sleep, bath and adornment."

[61]"The destructive lust of Venus is not accustomed to come to the couch of sorrow."

[62]"It is preferable to suffer in the stomach than in the mind, to rule the body than to serve it, to falter in step rather than in chastity." "Thus let her eat so that she may always hunger and immediately after food have the strength to pray and read."

[63]"Lest the body be stripped of its strength."

[64]"long and immoderate feasts displease me in the young."

[65]David S. Wiesen, St. Jerome as a Satirist (Ithaca: Cornell University Press, 1964), pp. 147-48.

[66]"Without food and drink love shivers."

[67]"Let your daughter get up at night for prayers, let her sing in the morning and let reading follow prayer."

CHAPTER V

CHAPTERS 44-51:

THE SUPPORTIVE MATERIALS, CHIEFLY MORAL


Having established in Chapters 42 and 43 the basic moral and intellectual features of his pedagogy, Vincent continues in Chapter 44 to elaborate the dangers of vanity, particulary with regard to excessive ornament of clothing, coiffure, and cosmetics.
Of importance is the fact that though Cyprian, St. Peter, Jerome, the Psalmist, Ovid and still other auctores argue against
any beautifying whatsoever, Vincent from the very beginning appears to offer a compromise in the word superflua,[1] which he repeats 'superfluum.'[2] The question which remains moot is this:
Is 'superfluous' to be interpreted comparatively or absolutely--
i.e. is too much ornamentation an evil or is ornamentation (art),
superfluous to nature.  It is necessary to point out that Seneca in Epistle 45.4 uses it in the sense of 'unnecessary,' as Jerome himself does in the Vulgate version of Ecclesiastes 2.16,
both of which texts were known to Vincent.  He may or may not
have known Caelius Aurelianus who used the neuter plural to in-
dicate bodily excrement.[3] Even if Vincent had a more moderate
view of the dangers of ornament than did his cited sources,
those very citations, by their number and vehemence of tone
would and do serve to undercut the force of any mitigating position.

Above one had pointed out the legitimacy, partial only, of
the equation of woman's chastity to man's prudence.  It is only

natural that chastity be directed against ornament, for St.
Thomas, in discussing the false prudence of the flesh, remarks
that "instead of serving the true end of all of human life, this
prudence is directed solely toward the good of the body and is,
according to the Epistle to the Romans (8.6f), 'death' and the
'enemy of God.'"[4] He further says that "prudence is especially
opposed to covetousness . . . covetousness here means . . . immoderate straining for all the possessions which man thinks are
needed to assure his own importance and station."[5] Vincent in
citing Jerome (who shows a rather unholy knowledge of such matters) deals with cunning, the obverse of prudence: "itaque de
curiosa vestis aptacione dicit Jeronimus . . . Vestis ipsa . .
. tacentis animi est indicium: Si rugam non habeat, si per terram, ut alcior videaris, trabatur"[6] and so much more of yet
greater particularity. St. Thomas writes that cunning (astutia)
is the most characteristic form of false prudence. What is
meant by this is the insidious and unobjective temperament of
the intriguer who has regard only for 'tactics', who can neither
face things squarely, nor act straightforwardly. In the letters
of the Apostle Paul this idea of astutia "occurs several times
in a contrast which helps to clarify it, for it is opposed to
'making the truth publicly known' (manifestatione veritatis, 2
Cor. II, 3)."[7] It is precisely this distinction between astutia
and simplicitas that Vincent is demonstrating by his quotation
from classical but especially patristic auctores.

There follows a long list of citations against the coloring
of hair and face, tints and rouges, the use of which is basi-

cally an offense because it is a reworking of God's own work,
implying thereby a dissatisfaction with the plan of the Almighty.
Yet Vincent introduces an added theme of his own to that of
painting's being wrong in its very nature: "Et revera quia de
consuetudine solent hoc facere meretrices, eo ipso debent ea
propter deforme testimonium omnino refugere et execrari puelle
nobiles ac sancte mulieres."[8]  What one sees here is still another example of Vincent's concern with image.  Reputation itself must be controlled, though he does not give any indication
how detraction itself, which seems often rooted in the best of
men, can be controlled.  Perhaps he is already anticipating the
next chapter which has as its subject the associates of the girl
and in part the theme of "by one's friends so shall ye be known."
At all events, Vincent here adds another responsibility to the
young girl--she must be as Caesar's wife--not only innocent, but
proof even against suspicion.

The very next sentence of Vincent reminds us again of how
it is that he knows patristic literature at first hand and most
of the classic texts only through the medium of _florilegia_.  Had
he the same degree of understanding as he has about Ennodius for
the earlier writer, he would have been spared some of the awk-
wardness and contradictions mentioned above.  Thus: "unde ennodius hiis qui non verentur talia facere sic loquitur, tamquam
yronice et irrisorie:"

> Tingite candentes roseo de murice vultus/Atque fidem morum
> pandite de facie.[9]

In no one of the classical citations does Vincent express any

awareness of irony whatsoever, not even in Ovid where it is so
very obvious.

Vincent underscores the notion of virgins' being free from
taint of detraction by specifying that in particular should
those maidens designated for the convent, i.e. for God himself,
be perfectly free. It is a fact true of the early Renaissance
as well as the Middle Ages, that those women who were well educated found no sphere of activity proper to them save that of
the convent.[10] "Denique virginibus deo consecratis omnino dis-
trictius talia prohibentur, nec illis mortale peccatum esse
dubitatur."[11]

Jerome is involved still further against the viciousness
of the beautifications common to women especially in regard to
hairdressing. The point is well taken, but one would do well to
recall that Jerome, valuable as he is as an authority in this
field, is remarkably ambiguous for he had recalled in his old
age "that even then he sometimes dreamt that he was a boy again,
dressed in his best toga, with his hair neatly curled . . . with
a sigh of relief he awakens, grateful that he is free from such
torture."[12]

All of the above may be interpreted as arguments against
cosmetic abuses peculiar to women, but there are serious comments which follow which are so restrictive as to prevent any
serious judgment that Vincent is truly a humanist. "Denique,
sicut iam ostensum est in tercio operis huius libro capitulo de
honestate cultus, non solum vitanda est honestis personis faciei
. . . vel corporis pulcritudo, videl, quia vana est et caduca

et eciam, ut in pluribus, nociua."[13] This view is the most ab-
solutist and completely self-denigrating of dark-age mediaeval
attitudes.  To compensate for this attitude it is not enough to
then quote Petronius and Tibullus, particularly the latter:
"Iuxta illud tibullij: sit procul a nobis forma cui vendere cura
est/et precium plena grande referre manu."[14]  Even though Quintilian himself thought that "Elegia quoque Graecos provocamus,
cuius mihi tersus atque elegans maxime videtur auctor Tibullus,"[15]
or even though Tibullus is singularly attractive for the sim-
plicity of his life and the modesty of his aims, still less
helpful is the fact that Tibullus himself is a conflation of
Tibullus and Sulpicia, mirabile dictu, although only about forty
lines, part of the Corpus Tibullus, belong to the daughter of
that Sulpicius Rufus elsewhere cited by Vincent.[16]  She is the
author of "the first poetry we have written by a docta puella."[17]
Certainly Vincent would not like to invoke the all-too-passion-
ate declarations of Sulpicius, but in his ignorance of the Tibullan canon, based on his use of collectanea, he has left himself open to the queries of later interpreters.

Further still in the responsibility upon women that Vincent
stresses, there is both his emphasis on motives rather than acts
as being sufficient for culpability and even of thought rather
than commitment as blameworthy: "Ceterum etiam, si nec appetat
vel appeti cupiat, sed indiscrete tantum et inordinate pulcritu-
dinem ostendat, laqueum aliis iniciendo mortaliter peccat. . ."[18]
This view seems radically limited, for Thomas at only a slightly
later date, was able to show that scandal is a complex issue in

which there are at least three aspects of fundamental importance. That is, scandal can be given, but not taken, taken but
not given, and both given and taken.[19] It seems clear that in
dealing with girls, Vincent glosses over by design or ignorance
these distinctions established by St. Thomas. In terms of attitude toward the relative responsibilities of men and women,
this omission takes on serious import. This tension is exacerbated by the following citation which combines the unjust and
the foolish in Judith: "Sicut holofernes statim captus est in
oculis iudith . . ."[20] The confusion inherent in Vincent's
quotation from the book of Judith has been cited above.

The conclusion of this chapter reinforces the defensive
tones of those sources which were themselves resisting the detraction and acrimony of pagan sects. Thus: "Et post: 'mulier
debet habere super caput suum velamen propter angelos' id est
clericos vel spirituales  viros, ne cadant per eam."[21]

The exact relation of arrogance and culpability is hard to
judge from the standpoint of our time. Less difficult to read
in terms of one-sidedness of the clerical position is the following: "Virginem ne conspicias, ne forte scandalizeris in decore
illius."[22]

Having exhausted the particular obstacles to a virgin's
sanctity caused by sensuous and sensual factors, Vincent in
Chapter 45 discusses the importance of companionship, of friends
as well as servants, but also, by direct implication, he is
counting on segregation by gender. The thrust of the argument
is that her associates are virtuous, so shall she be. In par-

ticular, the society of virgins should be kept free from married women. No intertwining of the virginal and matronly state should take place. Still worse is a mixing of virgins and married couples. The possibilities for a tension-filled triangle are obvious, but this possibility is but that of "Inter lascivas puellas et comatos . . . iuvenes . . . puella graderis."[23] The association of hair length and youth is obvious, but most clear-ly even beyond that is the idea that the example of the sexual roles of others is to be avoided: "'nolo'inquit,'te ad domos matronarum nobilium frequenter accedere, nec illarum tantummodo te cupio vitare congressum que maritorum inflanter honoribus, quas eunuchorum greges sepiunt, sed eciam eas quas viduas neces-sitas fecit . . .'"[24] And of course the most obviously danger-ous individual in the scheme is the widow:"Et de huiusmodi etiam viduis loquitur apostulus . . . 'adolescentiores,' inquit, 'viduas devita. Cum enim luxuriate fuerint, in christo nubere nolunt, habentes dampnacionem,' sc. apud deum repositam,' quia primam fidem, 'sc. voti prius emissi vel fidem, quam professe sunt in baptismo, dyabolo et pompis eius abrenunciando 'irritam fecerunt,' . . ."[25] The role of the widow will be discussed below, but the importance of that position vis-a-vis the maiden is viewed historically only in the light of the negative.

It seems that obedience to authority is a sine qua non for the pedagogy of Vincent. It is restrictive, but it is true. In order to support this position Vincent offers the anitpodal ex-ample on the negative plane: "Et post: 'applicaverunt quasi cli-banum cor suum, cum insidiaretur eis, et tota nocte dormivi coquens eos.' Si quis autem templum violaverit dei, disperdet illum deus. Ipso namque iure excommunicati sunt ecclesiarum incendiarii et etiam in sacrilegio et morti obnoxii . . ."[26]

Having offered the above it seems that Vincent is anxious to subdivide the aspects of chastity. Accordingly he begins Chapter 46 with the divisions of humility, silence, and fulfill-ment. Just what is meant by humility is a large question. Vin-cent quotes Bernard with approval in order to distinguish vir-ginity and humility: "Decet enim, ut virgo quanto est castior, tanto sit humilior."[27] Given that ambiguity, we are a bit sur-prised to find that 'silence' is so easily stressed: "'Malo,' inquit, 'sermonem virgini deesse quam superesse. Nam si mulieres etiam de rebus divinis iubentur in ecclesia tacere domi viros suos interrogare de virginibus quid cautum putamus, in quibus pudor ornat etatem, taciturnitas commendat pudorem?'"[28] Vin-cent follows all of this by an insistence that maidens keep their eyes under control. We tend to think of this as peculiar-ly female, but in fact it was an aspect of Bernardian monasti-cism that the monks themselves keep their eyes downcast.[29] Vin-cent goes on to support the importance of female silence and downcast eyes by appeal to both the Bible and Seneca, the better to argue a fortiori: "Hec Ambrosius. Porro de universa morum ac gestuum puellarium honestate et maturitate ponit exemplum idem ambrosius in beata virgine."[30]

Vincent concludes this chapter with a rather bold stroke: he offers a criticism of life at the court. Thus: "Sed quarun-dam puellarum urbanitas sive curialitas facit eas plerumque

procaces atque lascivas et dissolutas."[31] The general attitude
of Vincent which leads to compromise is extended towards a direct criticism of the ambience in which his pupils were to grow.
Whatever the condemnation of Vincent as a simple mouthpiece of
the status quo, it is important to notice that here at least
Vincent is so much in control of himself that he is able to indict the court for its bad morals and manners.

Chapter 47 introduces a whole new problem: that of the
movement of virgin to wife. Vincent does provide a very modern
proviso in his discussion of matrimony when he says: "Cum autem
ad etatem nubilem puelle devenerint, parentes earum vel custodes,
si causa legittima subest, licite possunt eas de consensu illarum tradere nuptui."[32] Vincent then specifies a wide variety
of reasons for marriage: "ideo dico si causa legittima subest,
quia plures sunt causa matrimonium contrahendi, videl, liberorum
procreacio, fornicacionis evitacio, inimicorum reconciliacio,
bellorum sedacio et si que sunt similes."[33]

One sees in Vincent of Beauvais the academic tendency one
associates with scholasticism. But most importantly one sees
that Vincent allows for independent judgment on the part of
girls: "Ideo vero dico de consensu illarum, quia sine consensu
nullum est matriomonium."[34] Yet this seeming independence is
quite radically qualified by "'Consulitur,' inquit, 'puella non
de sponsalibus; illa enim iudicium exspectat parentum. Non enim
eligere maritum est virginalis pudoris, sed iam viro desponsata
consulitur de die profectionis.'"[35]

Not only does one see a statement of why a girl's consent

is required: "Invite quoque nupcie solent malum habere proven-
tum"[36] which shows that Vincent is not thinking of the girls
themselves, but even more strikingly one finds that the girl's
judgment is required not with regard to the choice of her spouse,
but only about the time of the wedding.  There can be some doubt
as to Vincent's possible liberalism, but even if it lurks behind some subtle modifier, the examples and authorities he quotes
with approval again serve only to undercut any such putative
freedom.

As one might have perceived from the immediately preceding,
Vincent is more concerned about parents than children as is
clear from his adding to procreation and the cure for fornication yet another reason.  To the parent hesitant about bestowing
his daughter when he knows full well that "melius sit continere:,"
he says, "et illud apostoli, ubi supra: Qui matrimonio iungit
virginem suam benefacit? Ido quoque dicit potest opus grande
filiam tradere nuptii, quia matrimonium est figura grandis rei,
sc. coniunctionis christi et ecclesie."[37]  The logic of this
reference is that parents in order to be good symbolists ought
to marry off their daughters!

Of course Vincent will not have the marriage arranged carelessly for he stresses its indissoluble nature: "illud Mathei
XIX: 'Quod deus coniunxit, homo non separet', ideo cum magna
deliberacione hoc fieri oportet, ne postea contingat penitere de
hoc quod non possit remedium habere."[38]  Perhaps in addressing
his royal audience on this theme Vincent was recalling the celebrated case of his youth: that of Isabelle of Angouleme and John

Sansterre.  At all events he does point out by the vehicle of a
demeaning quotation for Theophrastus already quoted by Jerome,
a quotation one forbears to translate, that there is no school
for marriage and mistakes are inevitable: "'Equs', inquit, 'et
asinus et bos et canis et vilissima mancipia, vestes quoque ac
lebetes et calix et urceolus prius probantur et sic emuntur.
Sola uxor non ostenditur . . .'"[39]  Then it is that Vincent
rises to the level of intelligence one has been expecting of
him: "Et quod dicit de uxore, idem intelligendum est de viro,
sc. quod sponse non licet eum ante coniugium probare.  Et ut
dicit Ovidius in libro de remediis: turpe vir et mulier modo
iuncti protinus hostes."[40]  Accordingly great stress is placed
on discernible virtues in the future spouse which will increase
the probability of making a proper choice.  First are physical
virtues: the husband should be neither too old or different in
size.  Then he should be both wise and moral.  He quotes Ecclesiasticus: "Et homini sensato da illam:" then goes on to gloss
'sensata' in an intriguing way: "id est prudenti ac strenuo pocius quam diviti vel eleganti fatuo."[41]  Citing Sara, Vincent
lays great stress on parents and children and the obligation to
them rather than on the girl herself and her more immediate
physical desires: "Cum autem viro traditur admonenda est primi-
tus, ut consenciat non amore libidinis, sed obediencie filialis
vel desiderio prolis."[42]

Chapter 48 is explicitly devoted to a marriage course which
should be offered to the young girls.  Given the strong concern
for parents and the need for social harmony, it comes as no sur-

prise to find Vincent approving Jerome's quotation of Terence:
"Omnes socrus oderunt nurus."[43] The Bible adds to this classical view with: "Noli consiliari cum socero tuo." And why might
this be the first lesson taught to the affianced. Why; "Illos
igitur honorare qui solent odiosi ac molesti et graves esse, non
est sine virtute paciencie."[44] Only secondly in this hierarchy
is the girl urged to love her husband. She can manifest this
love in four ways. First, by being subject to him, as Genesis
had stated: "Sub viri potestate eris et ipse dominabitur tui."[45]
This subjection is itself manifested in three ways: by giving
him his due, presumably in terms of sexual rights, by fearing
him, and by serving him. Vincent again shows his concern for
at least partial reciprocity when he quotes St. Paul: "Uxori vir
debitum reddat. Similiter autem et uxor viro. Nam mulier sui
corporis potestatem non habet sed vir."[46] Then follows an erup-
tion of arbitrary numbering beginning with "Secundum est, ut
sollicita sit de viro" when one has had no 'primus'. This 'se-
cundus' itself has two reasons: "debet autem ei placere propter
duo, videl. ut ab ipso diligatur et ut ipse a fornicacione vel
adulterio retrahatur."[47] Three centuries later Ramus was to establish a logic based on dichotomous divisions, but Vincent has
no principle behind his statements that there are so many causes
or reasons for such and such.

Nevertheless Vincent does urge women to please their husbands so that 1. they will be loved, and 2. they will save him
from fornication. Then they are to overlook his faults and bear
patiently with those faults that cannot be overlooked. In order

to illustrate this argument he draws on Jerome for the _exemplum_
of Ylia, the lady who thought that because her husband had hali-
tosis all men must be similarly flawed.  This story is a popu-
lar one in the West, perhaps less a tribute to the popularity
of either Jerome or Vincent, but rather to Montaigne.[48]  In addition, wives should remain chaste willingly, not simply because
they have not been tempted.  Thus he quotes Ovid on the female
version of the Biblical admonition that he who has lusted after
a woman in his heart has already committed adultery. This stress
on thought rather than act is most unusual in Vincent, who is
almost totally concerned with words and deeds only in the ancient triple division of spheres of responsibility.  Thus: "si
qua metu dempto casta est, ea denique casta est:/ Que, quia non
liceat, non facit, illa facit./ ut bene servetur iam corpus,
adultera mens est/ Nec custodiri, ni velit, ipsa potest./ Nec
mentem servare: potes, licet omnia claudas./ Omnibus exclusis
intus adulter eris."[49]  Vincent then confuses the issue by offering two _exempla_ of women, the wives of Sulla and Candidus,
who are notorious for their actions not their thoughts.  In addition to protecting chastity by having a duenna for a wife:
"ceterum amor ipse uxoris in virum debet esse pudicus, que sc.
amoris pudicia consistit in tribus, videl. ut eum caste quasi
sponsum, non quasi adulterum diligat,"[50] indeed her attitude is
most important to the point where she may not use cosmetics even
to please her husband.  St. Paul is invoked as an authority for
the encouragement of sexual passivity on the part of women:
"'vult,' inquit, 'uxorem ad virum pudicam habere dilectionem ut

cum pudore ac verecundia et quasi necessitate sexus viro pocius
debitum reddat, quam ipsa ab eo exigat et opera liberorum ante
dei oculos et angelorum perpetrare se credat, ut eciam secretum
cubile ac noctis tenebras et clausum subiculum erubescat, dum
omnia petere dei oculis cogitat.'"[51] Vincent waxes a bit repe-
titious about the limitations necessary to a wife, but two of
the immediately following are illustrative:  first, a wife's
sexuality is a danger rivalled by the danger of her tongue: "In
muliere zelotipa est flagellum lingue omnibus communicans, id
est nulli a detractione vel contumelia parcens, de quo sc.
flagello dicitur viro sancto et quieto in Job V:  A flagello
lingue absconderis."[52]  Second, Vincent quotes with approval the
not so singular doctrine of Ambrose: "Hinc, ait, illa nascuntur
incentiva viciorum . . . "[53] The continuing criticism of cosmetics the use of which Ambrose suggests is worse than unchas-
tity is heightened by the exemplum from Ecclesiasticus of the
woman who is like both a bear and a sack!  Then follow the positive exempla of Judith and Esther who are used as exceptions to
prove the rule, although by their very moderation they qualify
the extremism of the preceding examples and judgments--and this
use of Judith and Esther is the work of Vincent himself.

Before his rather abrupt "Hec de mariti amore" which follows the idea that Queen Esther dressed richly only to satisfy
political obligations, Vincent cites the example of the morally
rigid Sulpicius Gallus--the Gallus who was the father of Sulpicia who exists within the Tibullan canon so frequently drawn
upon by our author.  It is yet another irony in a work oddly

full of ironies.

Having been taught to satisfy obligations to parents-in-law and husband, the girl is instructed to accept the duty of now educating her children, an education which like her own will be primarily moral. However, Vincent simply states this obligation in a single line without specific instructions regarding the nature of this teaching. He rather goes on to conclude the entire chapter with a sentence on the importance of household management. There is none of the detail and charm of the Menagier of Paris here and of course with Greek so rare a commodity in the Middle Ages, no Xenophon and his clear-headed treatment of the very same problem in Oeconomicus.[54]

Chapter 49 adds judgments regarding the leading of blameless life in general. Although Vincent draws on Ecclesiasticus to say that wisdom has always dwelled with certain chosen women, he adds to the responsibility of women the Caesar's wife principle that Jerome expressed: "Omni custodia serva cor tuum et cave de te vel contra te fingi potest."[55] He specified four defensive tactics which can be used against the possibility of detraction: "Cautela vero contra detractores est diligens sui circumspeccio, sc. ut non sit natabilis in habitu vel in gestu vel in conversacione."[56] While this can be tantamount to rudeness in some cases, it is clear that Vincent is primarily concerned with morals rather than manners. Thus quoting Seneca: "Efferat, inquit, matrona oculos iacentes in terra et adversus officiosum salutatorem inhumana sit pocius quam inverecunda."[57] Such speech as she is to deliver should be irenic rather than polemic in nature. And, of course, she must speak only when she has something serious to say. It should be clear to all that Vincent is now applying the very same standards of appearance and behavior to the matron as he had before to the virgin. Evidently the nature of woman and the consequent supports to it do not change, while obligation of variation in status demand accidental rather than essential modifications. It is vital that a woman recall that talkativeness only serves to hinder the moral growth of her husband. Accordingly she should keep in mind the example of the Blessed Virgin Mary who embodies the truth of Ecclesiasticus 26: "Mulier sensata et tacita non est immutacio erudite anime."[58] Significantly Vincent does not stress the sensata and erudite anime, but only the tacita drawing on St. Bernard to remind us that in the Gospels Mary is heard to speak only four times: "non nisi quater maria loquens auditur" and one of those times was to Christ when he was in the temple, an interruption, by the way, of his teaching. Vincent returns to the Old Testament to reinforce this example when he paraphrases the obvious crystal clarity of Proverbs 27: "Tecta perstillancia in die frigoris et litigiosa mulier comparantur. Sicut enim sub tecto in frigore perstillante non potest homo quiescere, sic nec um litigiosa muliere."[59]

In her general pattern of life she should avoid five particular vices: "videat ergo, ne sit maliciosa, sed simplex et bona, ne sit eciam audax vel procax, sed humilis ac verecunda nec sit impudica, sed casta, nec iracunda, sed mansueta, nec ebriosa, sed sobria."[60] The chief purpose for this excellence

of behavior has a great deal to do with the propagation of the
faith.  As such, Vincent in his zeal to bolster his arguments
by authorities, has forgotten in this case that the same problems facing them in their day were no longer operative in the
thirteenth century.  Thus he quotes Peter on the religious force
of wifely example both to spouse and to neighbor:  "Conversacionem vestram inter gentes habentes bonam, ut in eo quod de-
tractant de vobis tanquam de malefactoribus ex bonis operibus
vos considerantes glorificent deum in die visitacionis.  Hoc est
enim quod postea de . . . conversacionem lucrifiant sine verbo."[61]
Now gentes is used among the Fathers to mean "pagan nations,
heathens, gentiles."  In France of the thirteenth century there
were only Christians.  And those most in need of orthodox example, the Albigensians were heretics not pagans, so the first
Petrine argument here, which is directed not just to women but
to both genders of the faithful is not precisely apposite, unless,
that is, that Vincent was anticipating the Crusades against the
gentes by Louis, but even in that case it will be remembered
that the women stayed at home.  So much for Vincent's imperfect
sense of true parallelism.  He concludes this chapter by citing
again the five vices which are evil particularly insofar as they
are an offense against the male world.  Thus he quotes Ecclesiasticus 22:  "Patrem et virum confundit audax."[62]  All of which
theme is at the heart of his argument: "Hortanda est a parentibus filia nuptui tradita se ipsam irreprehensabilem exhibere."[63]

Chapter 50 deals with widowhood.  It might seem that Vincent was stirred by the number of widows (unknown as well as

celebrated) or that he was paying a particular attention to the
children's grandmother, Queen Blanche of Castile. However, it
is far more likely that Vincent was indebted to St. Jerome for
the stress on this state of woman as well as the tripartite division of maid, wife, widow itself. Jerome himself stressed
this category as heavily as he did for the very clear and obvious personal reason that the most important woman in his life,
Paula, was a widow and had been one for almost the entire period
of her relationship with him. Paula was the financial backer of
several of Jerome's schemes and just as importantly was a prime
confidante of that Church Father. Jerome could scarcely have
avoided the first state of woman, maidenhood, especially inasmuch as after Paula, Eustochium, Paula's daughter, had to be
guided into maturity. Jerome who had an almost Pauline attitude
toward marriage, nevertheless perforce had to speak of that in-
stitution at least to explain how we got from Paula to Eustochium. Vincent with his keen appreciation of symbolism, harmony
and balance in the midst of all these latterday widows, readily
accepted Jerome's trichotomous division with its equal stress on
the various responsibilities of widowhood. Frankly, one can believe that the French have always had a particular enthusiam for
maids and widows if not wives, for is not Jean d'Arc the virgin
heroine of France and did not De Gaulle adopt as his insignia
the cross of Lorraine and when he died what was it that Presi-
dent Pompidou said to the French people in announcing the general's passing, "Le général est mort; La France est veuve."

Particularly, however, Chapter 50 stresses the situation

of the young widow, who accordingly is presumed to be sexually
awakened and therefore just that much more a problem to God and
man. Vincent begins by editorializing on St. Paul in the first
Corinthians: "Mulier alligata est, quanto tempore vir eius
vivit; quod si dormierit vir eius, liberata est. Cui vult nubat,
tantum in domino. Hoc autem dicit non iubendo sed permittendo.
Permittuntur enim secunde nupcie, quamvis indigniores sint quam
prime."[64] He supports this position by drawing on Jerome in a
particularly ironic passage in which widows who are remarrying
are not to be condemned for after all even fornicators are for-
given! Vincent is particularly concerned with Paul's problem
that many young widows too easily take a vow of chastity which
they cannot live up to. Hence they leave the faith as well as
their chastity, thus becoming an embarrassment to the church.
He approves of St. Paul's remedy for this: "Et recte dicit
apostolus: cui  vult, nubat . . . Quod autem hoc dicat non pre-
cipiendo sed propter periculum incontinencie permittendo . . . "[65]
It is clear that marriage (and remarriage) is at best a remedy,
insisting with St. Paul that "quia melius est sive vidue continere quam nubere."[66]

Vincent follows this patristic commonplace with a quotation
which reminds us of just how fundamentally religious his education is. He cites Augustine for the standard hierarchy of purity: "bonum quidem susanne in coniugaili castitate laudamus, sed
tamen ei bonum anne vidue ac multo magie virginis marie ante-
ponimus . . . "[67] But he adds also Augustine's comment on the
logical extension of this principle" "Sed . . . quid, inquiunt,

si omnes velint continere, unde genus humanum subsistet? utiam
omnes hoc vellent, dumtaxat in caritate . . . multo cicius dei
civitas impleretur et seculi terminus acceleraretur. Quid enim
aliud hortari videtur apostolus, ubi ait, cum inde loqueretur:
vellem, inquit, omnes sicut me ipsam esse. Et post . . .Tempus,
inquit, breve est. Reliquum est, ut qui habent uxores sint tanquam non habentes . . . et qui utuntur hoc mundo, tanquam non
untantur."[68] In the very next paragraph this concern for the
eternal is forgotten as Vincent demonstrates some specific historical knowledge. He points out: "In primitiva quidem ecclesia
de viduis adeo ecclesie cura erat specialis, ut quedam illarum
sustentarentur de bonis ecclesiasticus."[69] In order to be so
supported they had to satisfy four requirements: they had to be
elderly, married but once, morally upright, and sufficiently
poor. Vincent again cites the familiar temptations which are
dangers to virgins and matrons as well as widows as he expatiates on these four requirements. Of course we have again the
danger of the male with curly hair, this time "calamistratus
procurator." Vincent seems to tire on this topic of widows for
he has less and less commentary of his own and more frequent
simple citations of authority and exempla as he hurries to his
conclusion, "hec de statu viduali." Just before reaching that
point, he stresses the obigation of families to care for poor
widows rather than having the church do that directly. We know
that King Louis established grants for the tuition of children
orphaned by his wars. One wonders if Vincent's "church" could
be read as "state" when it came to the care of the similar plight

of the women left behind as widows by those very same wars.

Having thus discussed the responsibilities for women as virgins, matrons and widows, Vincent is in a position to stress in conclusion the primacy of virginity over any alternative state. Thus he begins Chapter 51 with the view that for men as well as women virginity is the preferred state. He does specify: "Si vero nec puelle sit necessitas nubendi, nec parentibus eam nuptui tradendi . . . "[70] By so doing Vincent allows for political necessity, one of the grounds for marriage he had already cited, necessity which itself opens up the possibility of moral conflicts soluble by a casuist such as Raymond of Penafort. Jerome is twice invoked as an authority to prove that prelapsarian man was virginal and thus represented that state as ideal. Vincent not only specifies the supremacy of virginity over both marriage and widowhood, but he provides a ration of their relative importance. In the order cited it is 100:30:60. Indeed marriage itself is valuable, as Jerome has it: " . . . laudo nupcias, sed quia mihi virgines generant: lego de spinis rosam, de terra aurum."[71] Faced with the subject of married sexuality as an alternative, Vincent quotes Fulgentius whose grudging condescension is imaged in such an offensive way that one can understand St. Louis' pathetic behavior which we have above cited: "Nec dicere dubitamus, tantum a sanata virginitate carnis et spiritus fidelium coniugatorem, licet a deo concessum . . . distare concubitum, quantum similitudo pecorum ab imitacione discernitur angelorum. . . "[72] For mothers who might prefer that their daughters marry nice young men there is Jerome

with a truly wonderful trope so full of paradox--so easily a-
chieved when levels of reality are confused:  "Quid invides, inquit, mater filie . . . Indignaris quod noluit esse uxor militis
sed regis; grande tibi beneficium prestitit, socrus dei esse
cepisti."[73] Then follows the horrible example of Praetextata
who tried to draw her virginal daughter away from the convent
only to have her hand destroyed by a vengeful god.

Vincent subdivides the qualities of virginity into six aspects:  "sunt autem in virginitate sex commendabilia, quia videl.
ipsa est preciosa, speciosa, graciosa, fructuosa, victoriosa,
gloriosa."[74] To amplify the first of these qualities Vincent
not only quotes St. Matthew and _Ecclesiasticus_ in such a way as
to blithely overlook the sexual nature of the illustration, but
he also violates the rules of Biblical exegesis laid down by
Augustine by avoiding the literal which is itself meaningful for
that which is more metaphorical.  Thus: "De primo dicit dominus
in matheo xiii simile est regnum celorum thesauro absconditus.
unde dictur in ecclesiastico xxvi:  omnis ponderacio non est
digna continentis anime."[75] The thirteenth century is usually
thought to have been a century dominated by logic, yet Vincent
is rightly renowned as an encyclopaedist rather than as a logi-
cian.  Hence:  "Sed quia puelle habent thesaurum istum in vasis
fictilibus, ideo multe prudenter abscondunt illud in monasterio
se recludentes, ut servetur melius."[76] All of the above argument, as indeed the whole of _De Eruditione_, is dependent upon
a dualism of body and soul in which the former is always deni-
grated the better to heighten importance of the latter.

The second aspect of virginity, beauty, receives rather a brief treatment which nevertheless reveals more of the kinds of analogy which Vincent is content to substitute for strict logic. He begins by showing a certain measure of obtuseness that is quite obvious by the interpretation perfectly antithetical to the essence of a famous section of the Song of Songs: "sicut librium inter spinas, sic amico mea inter filias. Hinc et sponsus ipse ibidem inter lilia pasci dicitur, quia sc. in pruitate virginum sibi complacet ac delectatur;"[77] He then moves from lilies to mirrors by means of the one's pure whiteness and the other's reflecting of pure light. Thus: ". . . purissimus enim est candor lilii et maxime assimilatur incorrupto lumini, sic et virginitas illi de quo dicitur in libro sapiencie vii: candor est lucis eterne et speculum sine macula etc."[78] We readily enough appreciate Vincent's enthusiasm for mirrors, but we have here yet another example of the omnipresent dualism of Vincent's Weltanschauung.

The third quality is graciositas or graciousness[79] (in the sense of agreeableness, or at least as Tertullian used it) which is illustrated by two doublings of proof. In the first Vincent says that the virgin is doubly grateful for she is so to man and God and his angels, " . . . non solum hominibus in mundo, sed maxime deo et angelis in celo."[80] Implicit in this argument is the idea that the girl's behavior is being constantly watched by those above and those here below. Secondly, Vincent argues that Christ, both God and man, thus limiting the observers in heaven and on earth, was especially pleased by it to the point

of his having at his death brought together the most illustrious
female and male virgin in "Denique specialiter in beata maria et
in iohanne evangelista fuit christo virginitas familiaris . . .se
habere ostendit, dum eos sibimet ad invicem conmendavit dum ma-
tri sue dixit; 'ecce filius tuus', et discipulo:'ecce mater tua .
. .'"81

The fourth facet of virginity is fruitfulness.  Vincent begins by accepting the idea that virginity produces heavenly
fruit rather than earthly, supporting this view with a gloss on
Isaiah's eunuchs as virgins "quasi propter regnum celorum sponte
castrates."82  The 'quasi' is here important, else Vincent is
holding up Origen as a model of behavior.  However, Vincent insists in three ways even on earth: first, "quod virgines facit
liberiores ad serviendum deo;" second, "quod eos maxime assimilat
et familiares efficit christo," and third, "quod eos interius
unit" on the principle later enunciated by Bacon that he who has
a wife (husband) and children has given hostages to fortune.

Vincent expands his argument yet further when he comes to
considere the fifth quality of virginity, its victoriositate.
Imaging the crown given to the virgin as the first reward of a
struggle, the Christian Atalanta has reached a remarkable emi-
nence, for in her virginity she is not only like the angels but
"Et in hoc quodammodo virgines superant angelos quantum ad meri-
tum, quia quod illi sunt per naturam, isti acquirunt per victor-
iam."83  This is the most interesting principle which if exercis-
ed solely on earth might logically have given greater merit to
young widows than to virgins.  However, Vincent applies, if only

vis-a-vis angels, support which he gets from Jerome who provides
a masculine image of castration (and Jerome is the student of
Origen) to underscore his point," . . . quia contra naturam,
immo ultra naturam est non exercere quod nata sis, interficere
in te radicem tuam . . . omnem viri contactum horrere et in corpore vivere sine corpore . . . "[84] (Vincent adds to this notion
of difficulty another principle from Jerome. This selection
shows him even in the midst of this panegyric to virginity as
the maker of the realistic appraisal that virginity is for some
only, not for all.) In so doing he uses a more moderate Jerome
to undercut the more rigid view of Augustine who was only too
happy to see the increased rapidity with which the City of God
would come to supplant the City of Man if all were to become
virgins. Thus: "Si omnes, inquit, virgines fuerint, quomodo
stabit humanum genus? . . . Noli, inquam, metuere, ne omnes virgines fiant. Difficilis res est virginitas et ideo rara. Si
omnes esse virgines possent nunquam dominus diceret: qui potest
capere capiat, nec[85] apostolus in persuadendo trepidaret dicens:
'De virginibus preceptum domini non habeo, consilium autem da. "
Of course, Jerome is debating Jovinian here and uses whatever
weapons are at hand with the result, as can be shown, that he is
inconsistent on this point. Yet however inconsistent Jerome may
be, remarkably, even notoriously, it is Vincent who chose to
quote this passage and upon him is the responsibility and the
credit for this particular argument in the midst of a paean to
virginity.

The final aspect of virginity is glory, the reward for

victory.  As the psalmist says, there is glory for the saints in
heaven, but there is a special glory which attaches to virgins,
apostles and martyrs.  Vincent seems a bit confused on this point
for he speaks later of this crown belonging to virginum, martyrum ac praedicatorem, where praedicatorem replaces apostolis,
though how the one can be thought of as the successor to the
other is obvious.  This reward of the virgins is described as:
". . . denique triplici prerogativa dotabuntur in patris,"[86]
prerogatives which are located in capite, in ore and in pedibus.
Vincent's need to illustrate each of these habitations of glory
results in some confusion and elicits from him a singular ap-
propriateness of reference.  Seemingly carried away by his zeal
to satisfy this head to foot schema of glory, Vincent quotes
Revelation 14 about the 144,000 virgins who sing around the
throne of God, they, " . . . qui cum muleribus non sint conquievi
. . . "[87]  Patently there are the male virgins the example of
whom adds to Vincent's appreciation of the general virtue of
virginity, but it can scarcely be said to illuminate the argument which he is here making about the rewards given to the female virgin.  The very citation seems to exclude the theme from
this heavenly choir.  One passes over his continuing obtuseness
in regard to the Song of Songs, in order to stress the justice
of Vincent's quoting with approval from Jeremiah.  It will be
recalled that the ancient Hebrews put a high value on marriage
and stressed particularly the obligation of a man to wed.  Indeed there is no Hebrew word in the Old Testament for a life-
long bachelor.  Therefore, Jeremiah, whose virginity is a symbol

of the parlous times he cries out against, is singular as an
Old Testament prophet who espouses the celibate and solitary
life.  He is precisely the figure from whom Vincent would gain
the greatest rhetorical effect.

In a true anticipation of French history, albeit tinged by
his acceptance of Augustine's "he for God only, she for God in
him" doctrine, Vincent quotes a sermon of the Bishop of Hippo
justifying the honoring of virgins: "Quanto, inquit, fragilior
umphum, tanto maiori dyabolus opprobrio confusionis induitur,
tantoque mirabilior deus in sanctis suis agnoscitur, tanto eciam rex martyrum christus in pugnatricibus suis iocundius delectatur."[88]

In a final schema Vincent says: "verum de hoc ut virginitas
tanto fulgeat decore, quatuor oportet in ea concurrere, videl.,
ut sit voluntaria, integra et humilis et finalis."[89]  To begin
with, one gains credit for one's virginity only when one wills
it.  After quoting Jerome, Vincent points out in order to bolster
the argument's validity that "unde virgo fuit et ipse non ex
precepto sed propria voluntate."[90]  Having made this clear distinction by means of the example of Jerome, Vincent then quotes
Prosper on how even those who only are virginal by necessity can
gain merit.  This argument is subtle and sophisticated and it
comes near the end of a nearly work-long litany of simple dichotomous divisions: "Quosdam pudicos aut temperacio corporum facit
aut timor supplicii temporalis ab impudicie actione suspendit
aut occasio negata destituit.  Sed licet necessitate pudici sint,
non voluntarie tamen et primi, si. . . de beneficio nature sue

deo gracias agunt . . . et secundi ac tercii, si pudice vivere

consuescunt, in virtutem . . . de necessitate proficiunt et

paulatim ipsius pudiciie delectacione crescente pudici veraci-

ter fiunt."[91]

The second aspect is integrity, specifically the wholeness

of both the body and the mind in terms of their respective vir-

ginities.  Above we have noted how Vincent stresses the obser-

vable aspect of a moral act, i.e., word and deed, but here of

necessity he deals with thought as well.  Thus he lays great

stress on the wise and foolish virgins of Matthew 25 particularly

the latter, on whom he comments: "hoc est: habentes corpora in-

tegra et nitida per continenciam non habuerunt intus mentis mun-

diciam vel consciencie gloriam, . . . "[92]

The third element required is humility, but Vincent, show-

ing a thorough awareness of the ground that he has covered and

that he has covered exhaustively, says: ". . . sc. de humilitate,

iam superius dictum est, ubi actum est de morali puellarum insti-

tucione."[93]

Vincent concludes his fourfold schema of concurrent ele-

ments attendant upon true virginity and his discussion of the

education of women and the entire treatise on the education of

noble children with a statement on the need for ultimate per-

severance.  The last principle of pedagogy is that of competi-

tion and emulation coupled with a note of confidence, touching,

even if the words are by Cyprian, in his pupils' success.  Thus:

"O, inquit, sacre virgines, hortamentis excitate, emulis de

virtute documentis ad gloriam provocate, durate fortiter, per-

gite spiritualiter, pervenite feliciter, tantum mementote nostri,
cum in vobis incipiet virginitas honorari."[94]

[1] Arpad Steiner, _De Eruditione Filiorum Nobilium_ of Vincent of Beauvais (Cambridge: Mediaeval Academy of America, 1939), p. 181.

[2] Ibid., p. 184.

[3] _Latin Dictionary_, Lewis and Short, ed. (Oxford: Clarendon Press, 1962), p. 1806.

[4] Joseph Pieper, _Prudence_ (New York: Pantheon Books, 1959), p. 39.

[5] Ibid., p. 41.

[6] "And so concerning the strange fit of a garment Jerome says, the garment itself is an indication of the silent soul: if it has no wrinkles, if it drags on the ground so that you may seem taller."

[7] Pieper, p. 39.

[8] "And because harlots are by their habit accustomed to do this, for that very reason noble and holy women ought to flee and abhor this because of its unsightly witness."

[9] "Whence Ennodius speaks thus in an ironic and mocking fashion of those who do not fear doing such things: Paint your shining faces with pink murex and lay bare in your face the faith of your minds."

[10] William H. Woodward, _Vittorino da Feltre and Other Humanist Educators_ (Cambridge: University Press, 1897), p.250.

[11] "Finally such things are prohibited to virgins totally consecrated to God so that there be no doubt that they have not sinned mortally."

[12] E. A. Quain, S.J., "St. Jerome as Humanist," in the collection A Monument to St. Jerome, ed. by F. X. Murphy (New York: Sheed and Ward, 1952), p. 209.

[13] "Finally as we have shown in the third book of this work concerning the decency of dress, not only must honest people avoid painting the face and curling the hair, but they should not seek even natural facial beauty because it is a vain and passing thing, so that in many cases it is harmful."

[14] "According to Tibullus: let that beauty be far from us whose interest it is to sell itself and to bring back its hand full of gain."

[15] "Moreover we challenge the Greeks in the category of the elegy. Our own Tibullus is to me the most pointed and the most graceful!"

[16] Oxford Classical Dictionary, N. G. L. Hammond and H. H. Scullard, eds., (Oxford: Clarendon Press, 1970), "Sulpicius," p. 1023.

[17] Ibid.

[18] "But even if she neither seeks nor desires to be sought, but displays her beauty in an indiscreet and excessive manner she sins mortally by entrapping others in the noose."

[19] Austin Fagothy, Right and Reason (St. Louis: Mosby Company, 1959), p. 337.

[20] "Just as Holofernes was caught immediately in his eyes by Judith."

[21] "And afterward: a woman ought to have a veil on her head because of the angels, that is, the clergy and the spiritual men, lest they sin through her."

[22] "Do not look upon a virgin lest by chance you sin because of her beauty."

[23]"In the midst of wanton girls and long haired boys, girl, you will walk."

[24]"He says, I do not want you to frequent the homes of noble matrons. I want you to avoid not only those who are full of pride because of their husbands' ranks around whom crowds of eunuchs flock but even the ones whom necessity has widowed."

[25]"And concerning widows of this kind the apostle says . . . avoid the younger widows. For when they have become dissolute, they are unwilling to marry in Christ, having damnation i.e. being separated from God, they had disregarded their first faith i.e. faith of the vow first offered at baptism by renouncing the devil and all his pomps."

[26]"And afterwards they prepared their heart as if an oven while it tricks them, and I slept all night baking them."

[27]"For it is appropriate that the more chaste a virgin is the more humble she should be."

[28]"He said, I prefer the speech of a virgin be non-existent than excessive. For even if women are told to be silent in church concerning divine things and to question their husbands, what do we think about virgins, in whom modesty adorns their age and silence graces their modesty."

[29]Joan Evans, Life in Medieval France (New York: Phaidon, 1957), p. 62.

[30]"Concerning the honesty and maturity of the behavior of girls Ambrose offers the example of the Blessed Virgin Mary."

[31]"But with regard to some girls city life and court life have a tendency to make them insolent, wanton and dissolute."

[32]"When however girls have reached the age to marry, their parents or guardians can legitimately give them over to matrimony. if a rightful cause exists."

[33]"And I say, if a righful cause exists, because there are several reasons for contracting marriage: procreation of children, avoidance of fornication, reconciliation of enemies, cessation of wars and if there are any other similar ones."

[34]"Truly likewise I say, with their consent, because without consent there is no marriage."

[35]"A girl is not consulted with regard to the betrothal; for she awaits the judgment of her parents. For it is not appropriate to girlish innocence to choose a husband, but the girl is consulted concerning the day of leaving."

[36]"Also unwilling wives customarily produce bad offspring."

[37]"He who has joined his daughter in marriage has done well. It is a great work because marriage is a figure of a great thing i.e. the joining of Christ and the Church."

[38]"What God has joined, let not man separate, and likewise it ought to be done with great deliberation, lest afterwards one may regret what cannot be remedied."

[39]"He says, a horse, and ass and cow, dog or the cheapest things bought, also clothes, kettles, cup, pitcher are first approved and then bought. Only a wife is not shown."

[40]"And what he says about a wife, the same thing must be understood about a husband, namely that the woman is not allowed to approve of him before the union. And as Ovid says in De Remediis it is a disgrace for a man and woman just married to become enemies."

[41]"Give her to an understanding man i.e. one prudent and strong rather than rich or elegant."

[42]"And when first she is given over she must be warned to agree not from love of lust but daughter-like obedience and desire for children."

[43]"All daughters-in-law hate their mothers-in-law."

[44]"Therefore to honor those who are accustomed to be hateful and difficult and troublesome is not to be without the virtue of patience."

[45]"You will be under the power of your husband and he will dominate you."

[46]"May a man give his wife what is due her: likewise a wife to her husband.  For a woman does not have power over her own body but the husband does."

[47]"She ought to please him for two reasons: that she will be cherished by him and he kept from fornication and adultery."

[48]The Essays of Montaigne, E. J. Trechmann, trans. (London: Oxford Press), Bk. III, Ch. 5, p. 326.

[49]"When she is chaste because she is free from fear, she is chaste; she who does not do it, not because it is not permitted really does it.  In order that the body be well protected, the mind commits adultery and cannot be guarded unless she will. You cannot guard the mind even if everything is shut up.  You will sin within!"

[50]"Love of a wife towards her husband ought to be chaste. This decency of love consists in three things, to love him chastely like a husband not like a lover."

[51]"He says he wants a wife to have a chaste love toward her husband and give him his due with chastity and respect and by necessity of sex rather than exact anything from him and give heresy to the work of producing children before the eyes of God and angels, and even to blush at the secret bed, in darkness of the night and in a closed room since she knows everything is open to the eyes of God."

[52]"In a jealous woman is the lash of a tongue hitting every one i.e. sparing no one scorn or insult, concerning which lash the holy and quiet man in Job says: you will be hidden from the lash of the tongue."

[53]"Those incentives to vice spring up."

[54]Xenophon: Oeconomicus, Holden, ed. (London: Macmillan, 1889), p. 37.

[55]"Protect your heart with all diligence and beware lest anything be able to be imagined about you or against you."

[56]"But her defense against detractors is careful circumspection to not be conspicuous in dress, gesture, word, conversation."

[57]"When a matron is casting her eyes about to even a respectful greeting she may display a rude rather than immodest nature."

[58]"A sensitive and quiet woman is unchangeable in her learned spirit."

[59]"A continual dripping on a roof on a cold day may be compared with an argumentative woman. For just as a man cannot have peace under a roof in a cold drizzle, so neither can he with an argumentative woman."

[60]"Therefore let her see to it that she be not wicked but simple and good, not bold or impudent, but humble and modest, not impure but chaste, not angry but gentle, not drunken but sober."

[61]"To have your conversation honest among Gentiles, so that although they may criticize you, nevertheless they may by your good works glorify God on the day of the visitation. This is afterwards said about women in the same place that even if they do not believe in the word they will profit from the way of life of their wives."

[62]"A bold woman confounds her husband and father."

[63]"The girl must be urged by her parents to be handed over to marriage and to lead a blameless life."

[64]The wife is bound as long as her husband lives, but if

he is dead she is free. Let her marry whom she wishes in the Lord. He says this not commanding but allowing. Second marriages are allowed but are less worthy than first ones."

65"He says this not out of a rule but rather than the danger of incontinence."

66"It is better to be continent or a widow than to marry."

67"Indeed we praise good Susanna in marital chastity but we place before her the good Anne, the widow, and much more the Virgin Mary."

68"But if everyone wished to remain continent what of the human race--would that all should want this only in charity the city of God would be more quickly filled, the end of the world would come more quickly . . . the time is short. It remains for those who have wives to be as those not having and those who use this world as though they use it not."

69"In the early church the concern for widows was such that they were sustained by the Church."

70"But if there is no necessity for a girl's marrying or for her parents' handing her over, she is better off to remain single."

71"I praise marriage but because it produces virgins: I pick the rose from thorns, the gold from the earth."

72"We do not hesitate in saying that copulation of faithful married people if permitted by God differs from the holy virginity as a beast from the angels."

73"Why do you resent your daughter, o mother? You are unhappy that she does not wish to be wife of a soldier or a king; she has done you a good service, you will be the mother-in-law of God."

74"Six things are praiseworthy in virginity: it is precious, beautiful, gracious, fruitful, victorious, glorious."

[75] "Kingdom of heaven is like a treasure hidden in a field—a continent mind is priceless."

[76] "Because girls have this treasure in earthenware, they carefully hide it in a monastery to preserve it better."

[77] "Just as a lily among thorns, is my love among the daughters. He delights in the purity of the virgins."

[78] "Purest is the lily's whiteness and can be likened to pure light, so virginity is like her of whom it is written, she is the brightness of the eternal light and a mirror without stain."

[79] Charlton T. Lewis and Charles Short, A Latin Dictionary (Oxford: Clarendon Press), 1897 (1962 impression), p. 826.

[80] "Not only to men in the world but most of all to God and angels in heaven."

[81] "Finally particularly in the case of Mary and John the Evangelist virginity was familiar and pleasing to Christ. Because of this at his death he showed he had a great concern for them by giving them one to the other, mother behold your son, son, behold your mother."

[82] "As if castrated for the sake of the kingdom of heaven."

[83] "Virgins even surpass angels as far as merit is concerned, because what they are by nature these win by victory."

[84] "Because it is against nature, nay it is beyond nature to pluck out your root . . . to shudder at all contact of man and to live in a body without a body."

[85] "If all mankind were virgins, how could mankind endure? I do not fear this. Virginity is a difficult state and a rare one. If all could be virgins, the Lord would not have said: let him who can do, do it, nor would the apostle have hesitated in his persuading saying: concerning virginity I have no command of the Lord but I express my opinion."

140

[86]"Finally, threefold they will be given their due in the fatherland."

[87]"Those who were not defiled by women."

[88]"How much the more frail how much the more weak the vessel which triumphs over the enemy, so much more distressed is the devil and how much more wonderous is God in his saints and how much happier is Christ king of the martyrs in the women who fight for Him."

[89]"For this virginity to shine with such beauty it must have four things come together, that it be voluntary, whole, humble, and persevering."

[90]"He was a virgin himself and not from command but of his own free will."

[91]"Either natural temperance makes people chaste or fear of punishment keeps them from performing unchastely, or once the opportunity is denied it leaves them . . . but if chaste of necessity they progress little by little as the pleasure of the chastity grows and they become really pure."

[92]"Though their bodies were bright from purity yet they had no inner cleanliness of mind or glory of conscience."

[93]"Concerning humility about which we have spoken before, where we have completed the part of the moral education of girls."

[94]"O holy virgins, stir one another up with mutual urgings and call to glory with rivalled documents concerning virtue, persevere bravely, move ahead spiritually, achieve with good fortune, and remember us when your virginity begins to be honored."

CHAPTER VI

THE PLACE OF VINCENT ON THE SPECTRUM BETWEEN

ANTIQUITY AND RENAISSANCE

Perhaps the two most sensitive appreciations of Vincent's role
as an educator, and particularly his role as an educator of wom-
en, are those of Astrik Gabriel and Edward J. Power.  In the
former's view, Vincent "proves himself a worthy forerunner of
Christine de Pisan in pleading for the enlargement of women's
life."[1]  The latter makes two significant points: first, he
joins Vincent's name with that of Egidio Colonna to state that
the works of both "seem to anticipate Renaissance educational
theory, and it would be easy to transfer them to that period . .
. "[2]  Second, he writes, "it is true that Vincent touches on the
education of girls only in an appendix.  Yet the mere fact that
the girls' mental development was discussed ought to change some
conceptions of what mediaeval education was all about!"[3]

This study, particularly in chapters three, four, and five,
recommends some qualification of these serious and considered
judgments.  To take the points in order, Gabriel engages in both
rhetoric and some over-simplification based on hindsight.  It
is not in the interest of semantic polemics that one points out
that 'plead' is a verb laden with emotional commitment.[4]  It is
clear that nowhere does Vincent 'plead' in any sense of the word.
Further, Gabriel, having investigated the educational ideas of
Christine de Pisan first, has then turned back to Vincent in the
hopes of finding a tradition which flows to Christine. One often

sees that which one is looking for, or makes a world one hopes
truly is.  It seems that Gabriel has fallen prey to this natural
instinct of men and particularly of scholars, thus he makes Vincent an earlier Gerson on grounds which this study has found
neither solid nor real.  It is not enough to mention Vincent in
the article on Christine de Pisan only twice, once casually and
once in a way that implies a relationship only because they both
used the same form, forgetting that the form itself was so traditional, from classical times on, that it would be more surprising if they had used different forms. Thus: "The sorrows of
the invaded land  (that is, France by the English at Agincourt,
1415)  are reflected in her l'epistre de prison de la vie humaine.
Moved by the sight of so many taken prisoner, she decided to
follow in the footprints of Vincent of Beauvais who composed one
of the earliest consolatory letter."[5]  This will not wash unless
some further link between the Epistre and Vincent's Consolacio
pro morte amici can be shown which is more significant than the
simple sharing of a genre.

Professor Power shows a rare degree of sophistication in
combatting the once common simplistic notion of the middle ages
as some kind of nocturnal tunnel from which mankind suddenly
emerged into the full dawn of modern light.  However, this study
shows that the section on women is rather more than an appendix
inasmuch as Chapter III has revealed how much like a sermon De
Eruditione is, and how as a good preacher Vincent has chosen a
text upon which to enlarge.  That text is Ecclesiasticus 7:
"Filii tibi sunt? erudi illos et curua illos a puericia eorum.

Filie tibi sunt? serva corpus earum et non ostendas hyllarem faciem tuam ad illas," which are the opening lines of the work itself, repeated in the opening section on girls. It suggests by its inclusiveness that Vincent had in mind the integrity of his work from the beginning with the result that the chapters devoted to the education of women cannot properly be called an appendix. Admittedly, the number of chapters devoted to women is scarcely one-fifth of the total, though the number of pages of text is slightly more than one-fifth. The conclusion drawn here is that this ratio reflects the relative importance of male to female education, without reducing the latter to the status of a coda.

Based on research recounted in the preceding chapters, the principal conclusions to be drawn from this study are: first, without any doubt it can be said that for Vincent the education of women is not physical, only parts are intellectual, but primarily it is moral; second, it is clear that although Vincent is quite derivative in terms of his ideas, he is willing to qualify the rigidity of his sources whenever he deems it necessary. For example, in dealing with the danger of theater-going, Vincent is careful to introduce "non passim" which is a phrase remarkable for its temperance and moderation.

Yet with all due deference to Vincent for his qualifying of some of the more extremely restrictive positions of his authorities, it is still quite clear that Vincent is more concerned about the effects of a girl's behavior on others, whether family or society, than he is on her own soul. Further, he is

to invoke the principle of physical punishment for moral of-
fenses in the case of sexual extravagances. Although one is
often tempted to view Vincent as a Janus-figure, looking both
fore and aft, remembering the best of the past and anticipating
the issues of the future, here at least his gaze is firmly directed through the then present modernity of Salerno medicine to
the clearly dead past of Galenic authoritarianism.

With the above in mind, it is nevertheless important to
recall that not only will Vincent add a "non passim" when he
demurs at the rigidity of his sources, but he will also demonstrate a keen awareness of relativity in terms of mature responsibility. Thus he will point out that the dangers of embarrassment to family and society are not the necessary result of personal aberration so much as they are the likely effect of a certain age.

It is necessary to add that Vincent's selection of both
classical and scriptural examples is biased strongly in the negative, so much so that more positive examples, such as those
drawn upon by distinquished contemporaries like Albertus Magnus
are avoided. Further, the rather modern appreciation of the
value of play receives short shrift from Vincent who rather
steadily insists upon the need to control idleness. As for the
relative claims of temperance or abstinence as the center of moral behavior, Vincent is clearly on the side of abstinence as opposed to moderation, in such a manner as to underscore the
basically defensive and minatory quality of Vincent's rubrics.
It is a restrictive and protective moral education, far from the

Renaissance ideal of "I cannot praise a fugitive and cloistered
virtue, unexercised and unbreathed, that never sallies out and
seeks her adversary, but slinks out of the race, where that im-
mortal garland is to be run for, not without dust and heat."
This is, of course, Milton in his Isocratean Areopagitica, but
one does well to recall that this active and athletic notion of
virtue is the property of the Renaissance, but not simply the
Renaissance, for Clement of Alexandria circa 200 A.D. stated
that: "For from Zion will go forth the law and the word of the
prophet of victory on the theatre of the whole world."[6]

What is most clear from Vincent's discussion of morality
and intellectual training is that he is antipodal to the Pla-
tonic/Socratic view that the greater the understanding, necessarily the greater is the degree of virtue. For Vincent knowledge is in no way a necessary adjunct to virtue. Indeed, he is
much closer to his oft-quoted Ovid who felt that to see the good
and approve of it is not the same as to follow it. As for reading, it is necessary to remark that Vincent's first view of it
is not that it will enlarge the intellect or stimulate the im-
agination or even that it will lead to a greater degree of moral
behavior. No, it is quite directly and precisely that reading
serves to occupy time which otherwise would be a vacuum into
which the devil would happily move.

Vincent is a champion of the use of competition, emulation
and praise. In this he prefigures the Jesuits, but, unlike them,
easily introduces these principles into the education of girls.
Vincent does not specify exactly the age at which the boys and

girls will receive separate education, but he does state that the tutor of the girls is to be a man.

Vincent, moreover, demonstrates some sense of a psychology of learning in his judgments concerning the velocity at which a teacher should speak, but unlike Egidio Colonna[7] he says nothing about individual differences. Perhaps in dealing with royalty Vincent expected a kind of blue-blooded homogeneity. It is unclear whether or not Vincent used anything approximating the direct method of teaching Latin, but it is clear that for the better students at least he assumed a knowledge of both Latin and French. Vincent provides no list of vernacular texts. He also, unlike Jerome, does not provide an order of reading the books of the Bible which should be followed by the students. Of course reading is only one part of Vincent's curriculum for the education of girls.

Our encyclopaedist does offer suggestions for manual training in handicrafts, for both girls and boys, not an end in itself but as a means of concentrating the mind's attention on religion. More interesting as a device proleptic of the Renaissance is the use of notebooks, which Vincent seems to approve of by his citation of Suetonius regarding Augustus' practice, but he does not go on to develop any details regarding the aspects of that use. In addition to handicrafts, musical education of at least a limited nature is provided. That is, singing, specifically the singing of the psalms, is encouraged.

These more obviously intellectual or imaginative aspects of the girls' education should not blur for us the essential truth

of Vincent's position on female instruction: i.e., it is to be
moral. The most important aspect of female morality is chastity,
a virtue which he suggests serves for women the same function
that prudence serves for men. The gap between these two virtues
and the attendant invidious comparison of men and women in terms
of intellectual keenness and moral strength reveals clearly the
hierarchy in Vincent's mind. Accordingly, whatever praise one
gives to him for his moderating humanity, the limits of his attitudes are manifest.

Vincent believes chastity must be protected against various
sensuous tempatations, among which are warm baths. On the basis
of those elements he takes from Jerome, it is patent that he has
no interest in hygienic education. Cleanliness may have been
next to godliness for some 19th and early 20th century Americans,
but it was not a principle embraced by the leading educator of
thirteenth-century France.

The history of public (private) schools in Europe, particularly England, abounds in references to the kinds of food, usually inferior, which the students were to be fed. Vincent is
less concerned with the kinds than the amount, stressing the
moral advantages of fasting and abstinence. He is careful to
moderate these practices in the interests of preserving mental
as well as bodily health. In the midst of these practices the
girl's education does not stop at the end of the day, for she
is to be wakened in the night at least in order to pray, one of
the three aspects of Vincent's pedagogy.

Vincent's reputation for moderation and for looking forward

to enlightening aspects of education has to be qualified by reference to his strict attitude towards female adornment. He views the latter as a particular menace to chastity and only imperfect translations of Vincent's Latin have been able to produce a counter view.

One of the more negative aspects of Vincent's view of female morality is his placing upon the shoulders of the girl the onus of the Caesar's wife principle. The girl is responsible for both her own behavior and whatever interpretation others may place upon that behavior. It is a severe burden which only adds to the heavier responsibility Vincent gives to girls rather than boys in the sphere of moral action. Vincent further limits his rather inflated reputation as a humanist by denigrating the body's worth in order to heighten the soul as the focus of education. Commonly mediaeval as this attitude is, one must realize that Vincent is stating that corporal beauty is, by its very nature, an evil.

Vincent understood the importance of peer group influence, and accordingly is at great pains to specify permitted associates. For Vincent, homogeneous grouping is both by gender and marital status. Whatever the group or the individual, Vincent relies upon obedience to authority as a prime aspect of his educational theory. We have seen the limits of strict authority as an educational factor but we have also seen the weaknesses of the obverse, so that the modern reader need not take so superior a view of Vincent's position. Vincent's own obedience to the principles of his order, but his confidence in the superiority

of sacred to secular matters, allows him to indict his royal
superiors implicitly in more than one instance.  Further, one
should note that Vincent stresses words and acts rather than
thoughts, save in his discussion of the preparation of a girl
for marriage where the girl's desires are to be purified fully
as much as her words and deeds.  Vincent does state in a single
line that mothers have the duty to educate their children morally, although there is no elaboration on the ancient theme of
education, in gremio matris.

The once conventional opinion that Vincent's educational
ideas were based entirely on the works of St. Jerome is chal-
lenged and, to a great extent, controverted by this study: first,
because Augustine, Ambrose and other Fathers are invoked with a
sufficient frequency to become important influences themselves;
second, because Vincent is highly selective in the quarrying of
Jerome whose own inconsistencies admit of great problems in determining just who was the real Jerome.  This view preserved by
Gabriel goes back to Steiner, and it will be remembered that
while Steiner is of great aid in determining the classical references of Vincent, he is rather less helpful on Vincent's use
of Scripture.  This scriptural weakness seems to have extended
in part to the Fathers as well.

In connection with claims made about Vincent's humanism,
one recalls the distinction of Jean Leclercq: "The question in
reality is: do the monks owe to the classical, values which are
specifically human, with the power to enrich not only their
style and intellectual capital, but also their very being . . .

if humanism consists in studying the classics for their own sake, in focusing interest on the type of ancient humanity whose message they transmit, then the mediaeval monks are not humanists. But if humanism is the study of the classics for the reader's personal good, to enable him to enrich his personality, they are in the fullest sense humanist."[8] Without pausing to debate the validity of Dom Leclercq's dichotomy, one may nevertheless say that Vincent never indicates that he was studying the classics for their own sake in some belated manner of resuscitating ancient mores for the thirteenth century. Further his private delectation of classical aspects which are personally enriching is not at all evident in De Eruditione. By Dom Leclercq's standards Vincent is in no way a humanist. This study has demonstrated that Vincent was hardly a classicist, so dependent was he upon floriegia and glossae.

What can be said in honesty of Vincent is that he had a clarity of judgment and structure of opinion which were valuable for the totality of the conservatively mediaeval support which lies behind them. Indeed, one may conclude by saying that Vincent's principles of education are primarily religious and, moreover, that they belong to the thirteenth century. To the degree that they dealt in any way with the Renaissance or were anticipatory of modern education, we may say that it is not "that they do resolve or do not resolve the question of how women should be educated, but that they bring it up at all."[9]

FOOTNOTES TO CHAPTER VI

[1]Astrik Gabriel, The Educational Ideas of Vincent of Beauvais (Notre Dame: The Mediaeval Institute, 1956), p.3.

[2]Edward J. Power, Main Currents in the History of Education (New York: McGraw Hill, 1970), p. 315 and repeated by McCarthy.

[3]Ibid.

[4]Oxford English Dictionary (Oxford: Clarendon Press, 1971), p. 2205.

[5]Astrik Gabriel, "The Educational Ideas of Christine de Pisan," Journal of the History of Ideas (January, 1955), Vol. XVI, no 1, p. 6.

[6]Quoted by E. R. Curtius, European Literature and the Latin Middle Ages, W. R. Trask, trans., (New York: Pantheon, 1953), p. 138.

[7]Arpad Steiner, De Eruditione Filiorum Nobilium of Vincent of Beauvais (Cambridge: Mediaeval Academy of America, 1939), p. xxvii.

[8]Jean Leclercq, O.S.B., The Love of Learning and the Desire for God, Misrahi, trans. (New York: Mentor, 1961), p. 140.

[9]Power, p. 315.

# INDEX